OCCUPIED WITH NONVIOLENCE

OCCUPIED

WITH
NONVIOLENCE
A PALESTINIAN WOMAN SPEAKS

JEAN ZARU

EDITED BY
DIANA L. ECK AND MARLA SCHRADER

FOREWORD BY
ROSEMARY RADFORD RUETHER

FORTRESS PRESS
MINNEAPOLIS

OCCUPIED WITH NONVIOLENCE
A Palestinian Woman Speaks

Unless noted otherwise, scripture quotations are from the New Revised Standard Version Bible, copyright © 1989 by the Division of Christian Education of the National Council of the Churches of Christ in the USA. Used by permission. All rights reserved.

Scripture marked (TEV) is taken from the Good News Translation—Second Edition. Copyright © 1992 by American Bible Society. Used by Permission.

Cover image: Photo © Sara Marlowe. Used by permission.
Cover design: Designworks
Typesetter: Jeremy Keller

Library of Congress Cataloging-in-Publication Data

Zaru, Jean, 1940-
Occupied with nonviolence : a Palestinian woman speaks / Jean Zaru ; edited by Diana L. Eck and Marla Schrader.
    p. cm.
Includes bibliographical references and index.
ISBN 978-0-8006-6317-9 (alk. paper)
1. Zaru, Jean, 1940- 2. Palestinian Arabs—West Bank—Ram Allah—Biography. 3. Christians—West Bank—Ram Allah—Biography. 4. Military occupation—Social aspects—West Bank—Ram Allah. 5. Arab-Israeli conflict—Occupied territories. 6. Ram Allah—Biography. I. Eck, Diana L. II. Schrader, Marla. III. Title.
DS110.R324Z379 2008
956.95'2044092—dc22
[B]
                          2008017542

Manufactured in the U.S.A.

To the loving memory of my mother, Azeezeh Mikhail

CONTENTS

ILLUSTRATIONS

x

FOREWORD
Rosemary Radford Ruether

THIS BOOK OF ESSAYS introduces to the English-speaking world a very important voice for peace with justice from the heart of the contested world of Palestine. This is Jean Zaru, a Christian Palestinian from Ramallah, a Quaker who for many years has served as clerk of the Friends Meeting in that town. Jean Zaru speaks from the center of her being as a Palestinian Christian woman, committed to transforming the ways in which Israelis and Palestinians, the West and the Middle East, Christians, Jews, and Muslims have been taught to think of each other as implacable enemies.

Jean Zaru's testimony is twofold. On the one hand, she continually seeks to deconstruct the ways in which the Israeli government and the Western world misrepresent the Palestinian reality, covering up the structures of violence and oppression that are the underlying cause of Palestinian resistance. On the other hand, she constantly holds out another alternative, the way of being good neighbors who recognize the humanity of each side and their necessary interdependence with each other. Jean Zaru recognizes the depths of the challenge that she lives as a daily reality, not to succumb to hatred of the Israeli Jew whose overweening power rains down increasing humiliation and violence upon her people, but to protest this injustice in all its aspects, without losing sight of the human face of the "enemy" as neighbor and potential friend.

These essays represent the many talks that Jean Zaru has given around the world over the last twenty-five years. These talks have been given in many venues in Europe, the United States, and around the world. During this time, Zaru has served as a member of the Central Committee of the World Council of Churches, where she also served as a member of the working group on interfaith dialogue. She has been a council member of the World Conference on Religion and Peace. She has been a visiting scholar at Hartford Seminary in Hartford, Connecticut, a fellow at Selly Oaks College in England, and a participant in the Pluralism Project on Women, Religion, and Social Change at Harvard University. She has also served as a leader in the world, regional, and local YWCA. In addition, she is a founding member and leader in the Sabeel Center on Palestinian Liberation Theology in Jerusalem. Most recently, she spearheaded the project to restore the historic Friends Meeting House in the center of downtown Ramallah and create there the Friends International Center dedicated to building a culture of peace and nonviolence.

Since these talks have been given around the world, often to audiences somewhat ignorant of and conditioned by prejudices about Palestinian history and reality, there is some overlap and repetition between them. Again and again Jean Zaru finds herself in situations where she has to deconstruct these prejudices to try to convey something of what it means to live under Israeli occupation to those who have little experience of these realities. In some Western Christian audiences Zaru encounters built-in resistance to her message. Often these Christians have been conditioned to believe that their primary task is unilateral support for the state of Israel in order to compensate for the Holocaust and Christian anti-semitism. Any critique of Israel's treatment of the Palestinians is considered "anti-semitism."

Such Christians have difficulty rethinking this view and realizing that repentance for anti-semitism does not mean silencing the Palestinian story. Collaborating in Palestinian oppression is not a valid way of paying for their own historic guilt of oppression of Jews! Rather, they need to oppose injustice wherever it is happening, whether it be Christian oppression of Jews in Europe or Israeli oppression of Palestinians today. Our cause must be one cause of justice for all humanity, not just the silent collaboration in one oppression to pay for an earlier oppression, a mentality that simply continues the cycle of violence. This is Jean

Zaru's message that she struggles to convey, often to fearful and conflicted Western audiences.

Jean Zaru tells the Palestinian story through the lens of her own life and that of her family, her parents and grandparents, siblings, children, and grandchildren. Through the stories of her own concrete experience she tries to convey to Western audiences what it has meant to live in Palestine over the last sixty-five years. She takes them to the experiences of her childhood when Palestinian refugees were expelled from their homes and lands during the 1948 war and her family struggled to shelter many of these homeless people in their own home and gardens. She paints pictures of what it meant to be a teacher at the Friends School in Ramallah over two decades when their students had to live under curfew and interrogation by Israeli military authorities for nonviolent protest against occupation.

Jean Zaru uses her daily life to illustrate what it means to be ghettoized in increasingly shrinking Palestinian enclaves where one can no longer travel to Jerusalem, a mere ten miles to the south, for meetings, shopping, worship, or health care without the greatest difficulty. She shows us what it means for the Palestinian enclaves to be cut off from one another, to be unable to travel to meet with Palestinians in Nablus or Bethlehem, much less to Gaza, where the people have been totally cut off from Israel and the rest of Palestine for many years. Through her eyes we experience what it means to have to travel to Amman, Jordan, for a back operation, what should be a two-hour trip that stretches into two days because of long waits at checkpoints, and having to bump over back roads because Palestinians cannot use the main roads constructed for Israelis only.

Today this ghettoization of the Palestinian enclaves, or what Palestinians, drawing on the analogy to South African apartheid, call "bantustans," is becoming yet more severe due to the building of the "separation wall," a thirty-foot-high concrete barrier in some places or an electrified fence in other places, punctuated by watchtowers, which is being built to surround these enclaves, often digging deep into Palestinian land, cutting parts of Palestinian villages off from each other or from their own agricultural land and water. Just to go to Ramallah today from Jerusalem one must cross checkpoints where one sees this wall stretching in both directions around the Ramallah area, cutting it off from Palestinian neighborhoods in East Jerusalem.

What is the point of this constantly worsening ghettoization, impoverishment, and military siege against the Palestinian areas of the West Bank and Gaza, a treatment that fuels constant resistance by Palestinians, that occasionally erupts in violence, but is mostly expressed in nonviolent ways of protest and a simple insistence on continuing to survive in the midst of such daily repression? The official Israeli message, echoed in the Western media, is that all this is necessary for Israel's security. Without the "separation wall" Israel would be flooded by "suicide bombers." Without constant incursions into the West Bank to seize "militants" held by the thousands in Israeli prisons, often without charges, Israel would face constant attacks.

But this justification evaporates once one has actually experienced the daily grind of humiliation and repression under which Palestinians live. Clearly this repression itself fuels the resistance that occasionally erupts in violence. It evades the obvious point that if Israel promoted real mutual flourishing of both peoples, resistance would soon be replaced by a different relationship of cooperation and friendship. The repression seems to have a different purpose, a continuation of the almost sixty-year Zionist project to ethnically cleanse Palestine of Palestinians, to create an expanding state of Israel where Jews can be the dominant and privileged population.

Jean Zaru seeks to deconstruct and overcome many of the myths and misrepresentations that mask this actual purpose. One of these myths is that efforts for "peace" come only from the Israeli side, that there is no "peace movement" which originates from Palestinians. Underlying this claim is the assumption that Palestinians and Arabs in general are "naturally" violent and hence "only understand violence," a claim that has been a staple of every form of Western racism and colonialism of other people. This claim buttresses the view that Israeli violence to Palestinians is simply necessary and proportionate "self-defense," necessary for "security."

Zaru shows that in fact there have been constant nonviolent protests by which Palestinians have sought to oppose occupation. The first intifada (or "uprising") in 1987–1992 was almost entirely nonviolent, carried out through boycotts, not with arms. In my own experience the first peace group that brought together Palestinian Christians, Muslims, and Israeli and Western Jews to protest the occupation, was the Palestinian Human Rights Campaign, founded in the early 1980s by such Palestinian leaders as Edward Said and Ibrahim Abu-Lughod. Only a constant refusal to recognize the Palestinian nonviolent peace efforts sustains the myth that all initiatives for "peace" come only from the Jewish side. Zaru's founding of a peace center at the Friends Meeting in Ramallah does not begin, but builds on this long tradition of Palestinian nonviolent efforts for peace with justice.

Many Western Christians have assumed that some "peace process" has been in place since the early 1990s thanks to the Oslo Accords. They are confused when the realities of conflict endlessly worsen, and are often misinformed that it is Palestinian "intransigence" that is the cause of the failure to find a solution to the Israeli-Palestinian conflict. What they fail to understand is that this time of a supposed peace process not only entailed endless concessions by Palestinians, but that these concessions were used by Israel simply to push the Palestinians into tighter and tighter corners. Meanwhile the Israelis used the time of negotiation and since simply to confiscate more land, expand more settlements, and build more bypass roads, in an effort to make the occupation permanent in a way that would preclude the territorial basis for an independent Palestinian state.

No wonder most Palestinians have simply grown disinterested in what Western governments call the "Peace Process," since this has simply become an endless process of betrayal and increased repression. This process of betrayal also is key to understanding why so many Palestinians voted for the Palestinian militant party of Hamas in 2006, not because they wanted a Muslim state, but because they wanted leaders that might be less corrupt and compliant to Western demands for more and more concessions that would finally leave Palestinians with nothing.

Jean Zaru also thinks ecumenically and has worked extensively in ecumenical interfaith dialogue. Among the themes of her reflection is her relation to her Muslim Palestinian neighbors who are now the vast majority of Palestinians in the West Bank and Gaza, as Christians have shrunk to a small number in the Holy Land. The West has been misled into believing that the fading of indigenous Christians in Palestine is primarily due to the discrimination they have experienced at the hands of Muslims. But this is not Zaru's experience of her Muslim neighbors. On the contrary, she not only sees Palestinian Christians and Muslims as one people, but also finds much in Islam that is in harmony with her own religious vision.

Islam, for Zaru, is a faith that emphasizes the centrality of God in a way that rejects all idolatry of the human. Most important, it does not teach any kind of chosen or elect people favored by God over other people, unlike Judaism and to some extent Christianity. Thus, Islam is more genuinely universal. Although there are texts that can justify violence and also discrimination against women, Zaru does not see this as worse than these tendencies in Christianity and Judaism. All religions, for Zaru, are ambivalent, having resources for justice and peace, as well as potential for being misused for violence. Jews, Christians, and Muslims need to understand each other's best potential and work together for a more just and peaceful world. This is the authentic task of ecumenism in the Holy Land, and not a "Jewish-Christian dialogue" that ignores Palestinians, both Christian and Muslim.

Zaru speaks of her vision as "walking an edge where the spiritual meets the political." This indeed is the core of her thought as revealed in these essays. Unlike much of religious thought in traditional Christianity, spirituality for Zaru is not segregated in some private, ethereal part of the self, unconnected with the realities of politics, economics, and public life. Rather, spirituality is about the whole of human life and whether it is lived in a way that enhances justice, peace, and a sustainable relation to creation. The key issue is whether humans live with one another in a way that enhances loving mutual regard, or whether they seize power to oppress and marginalize others.

Zaru's spirituality is basically about converting our minds and our political relations to humanizing ways of living together, and overcoming injustice justified by false stereotypes of the "other" as possessing a lesser humanity than ourselves. For Zaru, this is the central message of nonviolence. It has nothing to do with passivity and meek acceptance of injustice, but is rooted in a resistance to evil that also called for fundamental changes in how humans construct their relations to each other. Spirituality thus has to do with every aspect of life, rooted in a vision and practice of love.

In this collection of essays Zaru writes not only as a Palestinian Christian but also as a Palestinian woman conscious of how women have been discriminated against in her culture and religion, as well as in most human cultures and religions. While discrimination against her as a Palestinian comes primarily from without, from the Israeli occupation and its support from the West, discrimination against her as a woman is often found closer to home, in the Christian churches, and even in her own family and close friends. As longtime clerk of the Friends Meeting of Ramallah and Christian leader both internationally and locally, Zaru should be recognized as a "minister" or pastor, a theologian and a church leader.

But in churches that only recognize a male-ordained form of ministry based on a certain concept of "clergy" and educational credentials, such recognition is rarely given to her, even in her own local Christian community. Many see her simply as a widow doing "volunteer work" who perhaps should immigrate to the safer world of her children who now live comfortably in the United States, rather than live under the difficult circumstances of occupied Ramallah.

But Jean Zaru is an important Christian leader for the Palestinian Christian community and for the world church. These essays represent a teaching ministry that she has shaped over many years from her base in her home and the Quaker Meeting House in Ramallah. Hopefully these essays will help make her voice and teaching ministry audible to the Christian world. Hers is a voice that we all need to hear.

EDITOR'S INTRODUCTION

Diana L. Eck

I met Jean Zaru twenty-five years ago, in 1983, when both of us were involved in the first stages of the interfaith dialogue initiatives of the World Council of Churches. It was on the island of Mauritius in the Indian Ocean off the east coast of Africa, an island with a multireligious culture all its own. There, about thirty of us from all over the world met for ten days of intensive encounter—Hindus and Muslims, Jews and Buddhists, an Ojibway couple from Canada, a Sikh couple from England, and the mixed lot of Christians.

Today, interfaith initiatives have become so common it is hard to remember a time when many in the churches were suspicious and uncertain about the value of crossing spiritual boundaries and cultivating relationships of mutual respect with people of other faiths. Today, as globalization has made the world ever smaller and religion has poured fuel on the fires of conflict, the urgency of interreligious bridge building has become ever more evident.

Twenty-five years ago, Jean already knew firsthand the challenges of life in a place where religious difference is tangled in one of the world's most complex and enduring conflicts. A Palestinian Quaker, she had lived her entire life in relationship with Muslim neighbors and she had lived her entire adult life since 1967 under Israeli military occupation on the West Bank.

During those ten days in 1983, our host was Anglican Archbishop Trevor Huddleston, who had been active for thirty years in efforts to bring down the apartheid system in South Africa. He had lived in South Africa for well over a decade and had seen it all from Sophiatown and Soweto—the bulldozings, the removals, the "hard-cutting edge of apartheid," as he called it. Now in his late sixties, he had been called to be Archbishop of Mauritius and the Indian Ocean. Soon he would return to England to head up an international anti-apartheid movement. He invited Jean to join him in this work. By the early 1990s, we would see the crumbling of the apartheid regime in South Africa, the release of Nelson Mandela, and, in 1994, Mandela's election as president of South Africa.

Twenty-five years ago, those of us gathered in Mauritius saw the nuclear standoff between the United States and the U.S.S.R. as the major threat to humankind. We wrote, "Today, the interrelation and continuity of life and death, of birth and death, are threatened and distorted by the sheer magnitude of the forces of death: the nuclear arsenals held in threat to destroy millions of human beings and, indeed, capable of destroying life itself." The threat did not evaporate, but in the late 1980s and early 1990s words like glasnost and perestroika came to common use. By December 1991, the Soviet Union was no more.

So much in the world's landscape has changed dramatically during the last twenty-five years—the end of South African apartheid, the fall of the Berlin Wall, the end of the Cold War, the break-up of the Soviet Union. Year after year, I would connect with Jean through letters, visits, and conferences. And year after year, as seemingly intractable conflicts yielded to change, this one great conflict between the state of Israel and the aspirations of the Palestinian people seemed to resist all attempts at an equitable, just solution.

Indeed, through these years, new tensions in the Middle East seemed to tighten the muscles of resistance to change. We saw the rise of religious chauvinism and extremism—Jewish, Christian, and Muslim—making the voices of moderation hard to hear. We saw the events of September 11, 2001, and their aftermath. We saw the emergence of a new American-led theater of war in Iraq, and we witnessed an evermore explosive Middle East. All this has happened in tandem with the birth and exponential worldwide growth of the Internet, linking cultures and peoples through constant information and communications and amplifying the impact of tactical violence.

While Jean remained faithful to her calling as a deep pacifist, it was clear that the conditions under which she lived became worse and worse. Leaving Ramallah to speak in Europe and the United States became ever more difficult. But even at times when her health was compromised, Jean accepted invitations to speak to church assemblies and human rights gatherings. Hers has been a vocation of active and watchful witness. She has seen the expansion of Israeli settlements, the strategic annexation of land, the gradual closure of Jerusalem, the first intifada, the second intifada, the multiplication of watchtowers and checkpoints, the construction of the wall, the opening of bypass highways for the use of Israelis alone. As an Israeli colleague and peace activist put it, "To watch the destruction—self-destruction—of an entire world, you need only ordinary eyes and the gift of not looking away." Jean has witnessed with her ordinary eyes, and she has spoken with extraordinary clarity and compassion.

Jean's truth-telling voice speaks to the reality of mutual dependence: Israelis and Palestinians are entangled in each others' destinies. Both live in fear. Neither has peace. Security, justice, and human flourishing finally can only be achieved together. Her voice for nonviolence has held steady, year after year, even as conditions on the ground changed for the worse. The voltage of Israeli response to her, however, seemed to grow. By 2006, even as she arrived at Harvard's Memorial Church to speak in a Sunday Faith and Life Forum, there were picketers from Jewish advocacy groups lined up at the church steps with their critiques. They denounced her for being a founding member of Sabeel, the Palestinian Christian Liberation movement, a group that advocates selective disinvestment from firms that profit from the occupation of the West Bank and Gaza. They criticized her language—especially her use of terms like "apartheid" to describe the policy of separation put in place by the Israeli government, with endless roadblocks and checkpoints and the massive wall it refers to as a "security fence." They recoiled as she described not only the actions of armed Palestinian youth as violence, but also the very coercive state structures of occupation as deep, systemic violence. These are hard things to hear for many supporters of Israel who have rarely heard a Palestinian woman speak in her own voice. Indeed, there are too few voices that bring us the perspective we hear from Jean.

I have long felt that Jean's talks and writings should gain a wider audience and I was delighted to find that Marla Schrader, who had been working closely with Jean in Palestine for many years, had taken up the task of transcribing many of her talks and writings. With this extensive digital record, Marla and I went to work, attempting to arrange what had once been discrete talks more thematically, taking into account the wide span of time over which these were delivered. Jean has been extraordinarily generous and patient throughout this project, offering help and suggestions at every turn, and meeting with us during her 2006 and 2007 trips to the United States. "Can you give me a reference for that?" I would ask her, following up as a scholar on the growing numbers of checkpoints or the number of olive trees uprooted. She was as patient as I was persistent. She has been walking the walk so long that she knows the history and dimensions of this conflict in her bones.

What is inevitably missing from the plain page is the spirit and the spirituality that suffuses Jean's presence as she speaks. Jean is a powerful peace activist and a compelling speaker. She is also a teacher, a mother, and an internationally known religious leader. She speaks out of her own experience and that of her people. As clerk of the Ramallah Friends Meeting, she is today the only woman to be the head of a Christian denomination in the Middle East. As founder of the Friends International Center in Ramallah, she receives countless visitors every month and very likely does much of the baking and hospitality herself.

I have learned much from Jean Zaru over the years, and so have the many people who have encountered her the churches, the academy, and the interfaith movement. It has been a great privilege to count her as a close friend and to participate in this small way in enabling more people to hear her.

AUTHOR'S ACKNOWLEDGMENTS

This book has been built by the endless efforts of many of my friends. Marla Schrader accompanied me for over a decade in my ministry. Her compassion, her dedicated commitment to the cause of peace and justice, her skills and gifts—all have been of great importance to me. I could not do what I have done without Marla. Global Ministries of the Christian Church (Disciples of Christ) and the United Church of Christ and have offered their partnership through their support of Marla throughout her years of service with me.

My dear friend Diana Eck believed in me and suggested that some of my work should be published. Her enthusiasm and endless hours of hard work have brought this book into being. Rosemary Ruether, my longtime friend and mentor, inspired me and taught me. To these three women I am very grateful.

I am also deeply indebted to my family and friends all over the world, those who are near and those who are far away, those friends of all faiths and nationalities who have accompanied me in the journey of my life. I have been enriched by each one, empowered in my struggle at so many fronts, and encouraged by their love.

With love and gratitude for all these gifts,
Jean Zaru
Ramallah
April 2008

1

WHAT LIFE DO I LEAD?

MY FIRST PROBLEM is always introducing myself. If I call myself a Palestinian, people first equate me with terrorism. If I say I am an Arab, I am assumed to be a Muslim. If I come from Jerusalem, thinking that this might make things clearer for my fellow Christians, someone inevitably says, "Oh, you are Jewish! Shalom." When I point out that I am a Christian, the inevitable query is, "Oh, when did you become a Christian?" I give the only reply I can: "I am a Christian, because my ancestors were disciples of Christ. Arabs were the first Christians. They formed the earliest Christian community in Jerusalem."

Sometimes this is a shocking revelation for Western Christians who hadn't thought about the continuous history of Christianity in Palestine. I continue to press my point. "My maiden name is Mikhail [Arabic version of Michael]," I tell them. "My father's name is Ibrahim [Arabic version of Abraham]. My grandfather is Musa [Arabic form of Moses]. My brother's name is John. My uncles are Isaac, Jacob, Jad, and David, and my grandmother's name is Sarah."

So I am a Palestinian, a Palestinian woman, a Palestinian Christian woman, and I am also a Quaker and pacifist. Identity is always complex.

As a Palestinian, I am one of about nine million Palestinians both inside and outside Palestine, struggling for justice and freedom for our homeland. Half of our Palestinian people have been uprooted and forcibly thrown out of their homes, some more than once, and the other half subjected to the rule of others in our own land. Yet, Palestinians are viewed primarily as "a problem" for many in Israel because they want the land without the people. From our standpoint, we are denied the right to self-determination and live under Israeli military occupation, which is the root cause of other forms of human rights violations against us. Many of my people have no guarantees of basic life necessities and no hope for the full development of their human potential. So as a people and as a nation, we are seeking equality, justice, and freedom.

As a Palestinian woman in a male-dominated culture there are other issues. I don't enjoy equality with my brothers. In my culture, as in many others, girls traditionally have not had equal opportunities for education and health care, although this is beginning to change. On the whole, girls are supposed to serve and to conform. They are often looked down upon if they choose a life that is different from what society expects. There is always a double standard of judgment when it comes to boys and girls.

As an ordinary married woman with limited financial resources, I had to work outside the home for extra income. At the same time, however, I had to break my back to be a traditional homemaker so I would not lose credibility. And I volunteered, giving time to the YWCA and to other women's organizations so as to convince other women that it is possible to be involved in social issues, to convince other women that their voices count, and to convince them that volunteers are not only the affluent who can afford to volunteer and are bored staying home. As for my volunteer work in the church, people constantly asked, "Why would a woman, a layperson, a happily married young mother like me be involved with religion and churches?" Their presumption was that religion is either the work of men or the work of single, old, or widowed women who have no life of their own.

Not only am I a Palestinian and a woman, but I am also a Christian. My non-Christian neighbors turn to me, seeking an explanation to what is going on when the Bible is used to justify the dispossession of our people. Who are these Western Christian Zionists who come to supply Jewish claims to our land? And I feel responsible as a Christian to speak

2

out when other Christians abuse the Bible to justify the worship of the false gods and idols of today, to justify the submission of women, or to demonize non-Christian neighbors, whether Muslim or Jewish.

As a Christian living in the Holy Land, I have seen the whole spectrum of Christian churches firsthand. I have seen how different Western churches, interested in their so-called presence in the Holy Land, have divided us with their numerous denominations and made many Palestinian Christians somehow feel inferior, patronized, and alienated from our own culture and language. Loyalty is expected to a foreign religious leadership in Rome, England, Greece, Germany, or the United States.

It is often a struggle simply to affirm my own identity and that of my people, to affirm the presence of some twelve million Arab Christians in the Middle East. Everyone has an agenda that they bring to my identity as a Palestinian Christian. For liberal Christians, influenced by post-Holocaust theology and European history and guilt, I am simply not on their agenda as a Palestinian Christian. My voice strikes a discordant note in an already difficult dialogue between Christians and Jews. My very existence disturbs the balance. For fundamentalist Christians and Christian Zionists, I am among those who reject their view of history and the Bible. The International Christian Embassy in Jerusalem is the most overt political supporter of Israel on the ground. It is pro-Israel politically but anti-Jewish theologically. As a Palestinian Christian, I am invisible in this rendering of things; I am completely absent from the theological picture of such Christians, but considered as part of the cursed who are standing in the way of the fulfilment of the prophecy of God.

Although we are the modern heirs of the disciples of Jesus in Jerusalem and despite our rich contribution to the Middle East, Palestinian Christians have become unknown, unacknowledged, and forgotten by much of the world. We are a highly educated community with deep historical roots, a community that is, unfortunately, diminishing every day as a result of political and economic pressures. Our future is uncertain; the pressures are enormous.

As a Quaker, I have to struggle on yet another front, for I am labeled as a "pacifist," and this is misinterpreted as being passive or submissive or even accepting of the injustice we experience as victims of violence. It is not easy to be a pacifist when people see that violence seems to bring about change and nonviolence seems to permit our homeland and our rights to be given to others. It is not easy to explain nonviolence in a continually violent conflict, yet to me it seems the obvious and only path, and many Palestinians through the years have chosen it.

So this is the complexity of my identity: an Arab, a Palestinian, a Christian, a Quaker, a woman.

The Generations of War: Telling Our Stories

Storytelling makes the world stronger because stories reveal the complexity of our truth. By telling our stories, we resist the diminishing of the reality of our lives. We resist vague and generalized abstractions and we maintain the urgency and intensity of the concrete. And so I share with you something of my story in the hopes of revealing the complexity of our truth.

In the war of 1948, I was only eight years old. Yet I can remember the fear very clearly. I remember hiding in the basement in our home. I remember the refugees coming to Ramallah from the coastal plain of Palestine. I remember how my father and my older brother, hearing of the plight of refugees in the coastal plains, took a truck with water and bread and drove west to deliver supplies and to pick up women and children who were running away from the dangers of war but could not go on walking. Fifty of these people shared our house for a period of six weeks. Another one hundred camped under our pine trees. Our Friends Meeting House in Ramallah sheltered many more families until they found a way of settling somewhere else. I have lived most of my life next to a refugee camp. That war ended, but the plight of those refugees continues. A fourth generation of refugees has now been born in that camp.

As a girl, I went to the Friends School in Ramallah, a school that had been established by the Quakers for the education of girls. My older sister and brother were already in the United States attending college. Although I had been accepted to Bryn Mawr College and paid my registration fees, I realized that the economic burden and the uprooted-ness was too much for my family to bear. After I graduated from school, I was engaged to be married to the man who had been the chemistry teacher in the Friends School, Fuad Zaru. He later became the principal of the school, and we lived on the school campus for many years until his death in 1987. My interest and joy in learning and my husband's encouragement helped me to pursue knowledge until this day.

By the time war broke out again in 1967, our oldest son was eight years old. His sister was five. We were hiding in a shelter, which was partially damaged, and our very lives were threatened at every moment. As the bombs fell, our shelter became more and more precarious. Then we moved to another shelter, which we shared with thirty children and adults. That night, two little girls died from an Israeli air raid. Overnight, we found ourselves under the dominance of an occupying power. To many, the evil of war is now considered preferable to the evil of military occupation and foreign domination. I remember, and now I understand, why my aunt from Nazareth wept when we rejoiced that the 1967 war had ended. She told us, "I have lived in Nazareth since 1948 and the war has not ended. What is coming will be worse."

Four of my seven grandchildren were born during the first intifada, which lasted from 1987 to 1991. One of them was six years old during the Gulf War in 1991. When I look back on these years, these decades, I wonder how much longer we have to live with the experiences of war that seem to go on from one generation to the next. I was a child when it all began. Now I am a grandmother. I have lived under Israeli military occupation for more than half of my life.

During the beginning of the first intifada my oldest son Saleem's wedding was scheduled for February 7, 1988. Two days before the wedding we learned that the seventh would be a day of mourning because of the many Palestinians who had been killed. So on the fifth our family sat together with the family of Saleem's fiancé, Carol, and decided to have the wedding at our home that very evening. We had four hours to get things ready, from 4:00 p.m. to 8:00 p.m. that day. The small wedding at home with only about a hundred people attending turned out to be beautiful. Landrum Bolling, a longtime Quaker peace activist, presided over the ceremony. In Palestine, even a wedding cannot be planned as scheduled!

When my daughter got engaged during the invasion of Lebanon in 1982, we had to cancel the reception and any festive celebrations in solidarity with our people. When I learned with great joy that I was going to be a grandmother, I kept my fears to myself. Many women aborted from tear-gas bombs, and my children and I were worried.

My neighbors and even my family often ask me why I keep working for peace and justice against seemingly hopeless odds. The only thing I can say is that this is my faith, a practical, everyday faith. One of the posters in our home in Ramallah reads, "True Godliness doesn't turn people out of this world but enables them to live better in it and excites their endeavors to mend it." How true these words are to me, for I learned through my life and through spiritual struggle that my faith is a practical faith. It is what helps me to endure year after year. It is what helps me try to love all women and men, even those who violate my dignity and human worth. It is such a challenge, and it is my lifelong work.

In the days before he died, my husband gathered the family together three times and said, "I am very proud of Jean's work and accomplishments. I want you to support her in going on with the path that she has chosen." My husband, my father, and my brother were three men in my life who encouraged me in my struggle on many fronts. Unfortunately, none of them are alive today, but they left me legacies that encouraged me to go on even in the darkest moments. My mother has also been a great support by helping me when my hands were full. She has taken care of my children, helped out when I traveled to different parts of the world, and encouraged me when I was tired and anxious.

For forty years, I have been walking that edge where the spiritual meets the political. For me, the two have always been integrated. My spirituality is rooted in the human dignity and human rights of all people, and the sacredness of Mother Earth. I feel compelled to work for a world in which human freedom and dignity can flourish. Spirituality can bring life and vibrancy and imagination to my struggle, but of course I recognize that the mixture of religion and politics can also fuel the most extreme and violent acts and lead to systems of self-righteous repression.

Many activists mistrust religion and spirituality, sometimes for good reason. But each of us finds ourselves engaged in the work for peace and justice because something is sacred to us—so sacred that it means more than convenience or comfort. It might be God, or the Spirit, or the sacredness of life or belief in freedom. Whatever it is, it can nurture us.

Many people want religion, but they want it in its place apart from their business, their politics, their luxuries and conveniences. My own experience is that religion cannot be lived except with one's whole everyday life, and what cannot be humanly lived is not religion. Religion involves commitment and relationship, and relationship is action and engagement in the real issues of life. But there is no relationship without love, only waste, strife, madness, and destruction. Love makes it necessary to find the way of truth, understanding, justice, and peace. My kind of religion is a very active, highly political, often controversial, and sometimes very dangerous form of engagement in active nonviolence for the transformation of our world.

Teaching

For eighteen years, my husband was principal of the Friends School in Ramallah and I was a teacher of fourth- and fifth-grade boys and high school girls. The Friends School was our home and our life. For me, teaching was a way of doing something constructive in a situation in which military force seemed to have determined the status quo and peaceful settlement seemed a hopeless dream.

I developed an ethics curriculum for my classes of Muslim and Christian students and a home economics class. My challenge was great and my job was not easy. Through my classes, I learned more about my own values and myself. I tried to bring Christians and Muslims closer by building a new community of relationship with each other, transcending differences of ideology, class, and faith.

Most of the students in our school have Arabic names, and many of those are names of prophets, famous leaders, values, or virtues. By learning about our own names and namesakes, students can see how close the different religious traditions and values are to each other and can clarify in their own lives if they want to live by these values.

7

Once when I went to class, the students were shouting, "PLO! Israel No!" I could not stop them because I value freedom of expression if we are to solve problems. But I was afraid that if they went on, the Israeli soldiers would throw tear-gas bombs or arrest them. They were only in fourth and fifth grade, and I cared for their safety. So I went over and wrote "PLO" on the blackboard. There was dead silence. They knew that few teachers would have the courage to write this. It was illegal then for Palestinians to mention the PLO, to use the Palestinian flag, or even use the colors of the flag. I asked, "Do you know what the letters really stand for?" "No," they replied. Then I explained what the verb *liberate* really means. I asked them to write down five things from which they would like to liberate themselves, our country, and our world. I learned a lot through them and we all learned about the different types of captivities that we experience. We are all captives—either because of our choices or our ignorance, or the choices and ignorance of others. We are all in need of liberation.

In my classes with these boys, I also tried to introduce the issue of gender roles. From them, I learned how they saw the status of their mothers. I asked each boy to draw a picture of something or someone that represents continuous, steady, faithful work. Two-thirds of them drew pictures of their mothers. What can we do to change the fact that women actually do so much of the constant work? "By helping more," they volunteered. But they added that they met lots of opposition from fathers and aunts at home if they helped their mothers out. That is not their duty, they would be told. One boy actually cried when he told us, "I didn't help my mother, because my aunt cursed me and scolded my mother. What shall I do?" I had to think for a few minutes and I knew I was starting a domestic revolution. I asked the boy, "What is more shameful—to help your mother or to see her suffering under her load of work?" We then looked at the ways mothers are spoken of in the Qur'an and in the Bible.

With my eleventh- and twelfth-grade home economics students, I always started out in my course by asking them to write a paper on how they will make responsible decisions when they plan meals, buy clothes, or run a household. This legitimized a whole set of questions about what it means to live responsibly—in relation to oneself, one's family, and the wider Palestinian community. What we buy and eat is important. Starting our meals from scratch is not only healthier and cheaper, but by buying local products, we help the simple farmer to stay on the land and not move to the city. We avoid the problems of waste or preservatives in processed foods. We avoid using products made by Israel, which are highly taxed. We cannot pray for peace and pay for war. The same is true with clothes. Why buy ready-made clothes when we have wonderful dressmakers, when we have women who knit at home for a living? We have to support them. All this may not bring about overnight change, but it empowered my students. It gave them a sense of worth and dignity. Their lives and choices count and so do the lives and choices of other women.

How do I teach a culture of nonviolent action? First, I raise critical and decisive consciousness—consciousness of the value of justice over against injustice, peace over against warfare, humane institutions over against dehumanizing institutions. I try to make it very clear that we are working against evil and not against people. Human well-being is our ultimate goal, and we should be ready to say what we think is the truth and be ready to pay the price.

The biggest obstacle to personal growth and to working for peace is feeling powerless or hopeless. The most important thing I could impart in my classes, then, was a sense of empowerment, a sense of competence to make decisions about how we want to live, and a sense of optimism about the future. While we do not know what the future holds, we do know that we hold the future in our hands. Affirmation is a future-oriented strategy. I affirm what is good and beautiful in our culture, our values, our food, our family relations, our arts, and our embroidery. I use affirmation instead of negativity, even though there is so much that I reject. This gave my students more self-esteem and made it easier for them to see the good in others, including those with whom we are in conflict.

My students now know that to violate is not only to use force but to treat others who are sacred children of God as nothing. No matter how we are treated, we must not treat anyone else as nothing or less worthy than ourselves. It is not easy for us to learn to think of the sacredness of life and human dignity when our dignity and worth is rarely recognized. But through the hurt, the pain, and the wounds we must try to realize our power and become real agents of change. Real change is not simply transferring power from one group to the other, but changing the relationship between us. It might be a dream but it is my human right to dream and to work toward the reality of this dream.

Traveling

My ecumenical and international involvement requires that I travel—mostly to countries in Europe and to the United States. When I worked with the World Council of Churches, the World Conference on Religion and Peace, or the World YWCA, I needed to travel to attend meetings. But for me, even in this age of highways and jets, traveling has always been an ordeal.

Since 1967, every time I needed to go to Amman, Jordan, for one reason or another, I had to cross the King Hussein Bridge on the River Jordan. It is the one bridge that West Bank Palestinians are permitted by the state of Israel to use to exit our country. Crossing this bridge is not like crossing American bridges in your cars, just waiting to pay the tolls. For us, it is leaving occupied Palestine, which requires securing military permits, paying expensive fees, and being thoroughly checked—our papers, our identity cards and our passports, our bodies—often without any respect for our human dignity.

It should take less than one hour to reach the bridge from Ramallah. In the past few years, however, it has taken five to six hours just to reach the bridge, since we are not permitted to travel on the highways that Israeli settlers use, but have to use secondary roads with dozens of checkpoints, detours, and roadblocks. It takes at least thirteen hours in total to cross the border itself and subsequently arrive in Amman. I can fly from Amman to New York in the same amount of time!

It is hard to describe the heavy tolls we have paid at this bridge—our health, our separation from loved ones, our anxieties both about leaving and hoping to return. They have checked our bodies, our shoes, and our belongings piece by piece. Throughout the last nearly forty years, Israel claimed that these severe measures were for security. I always wondered whether, through all their devices, they could check the hearts and minds of the Palestinians? Could they see how we felt? Could they notice our pain? Or is this not part of the security check? Or part of building bridges with neighbors whose lives are entwined with their own?

Looking at the people around me during the long waiting hours at the checkpoint or in the bus listening to their conversations, I hear individual stories of pain, of families being torn apart, of despair and suffering, longing and hope. The tolls we all pay are many. Traveling under occupation drains our lives, impairs our health, adds to our financial burden, and increases our separation anxieties, as neither leaving nor returning is ever guaranteed.

Often as I wait with the others I feel like shouting to the Israeli authorities, "We ourselves, we tell you, are sacred human beings. Why do you treat us this way?" Or sometimes I feel like repeating the words of Psalm 22:1-2, "My God, my God, why have you forsaken me? Why are you so far from helping me, from the words of my groaning? O my God, I cry by day, but you do not answer; and by night, but find no rest."

It is not surprising that when I arrive at my destination, I am often exhausted by the ordeal of traveling. Organizers ask me for my travel expenses in the United States. I can submit the cost of an airline ticket, but can I put a price on the pain, the humiliation, the fatigue, and the anxiety?

This is not a personal issue. This is a structural issue that is part of a much wider problem—the systematic attempt to inhibit the movement of Palestinians in the West Bank, Gaza, and East Jerusalem, which is a basic human right, through countless barriers, checkpoints, ditches, and fences. It is part of the systematic attempt to fragment our people and batter our souls.

Leaving Palestine

Palestinians would not leave if they could stay, but many Palestinians have no choice but to leave their country. Let me tell you about my own family and, more generally, about the people of Ramallah, a town settled some four hundred years ago by seven Arab Christian families.

My maiden name is Mikhail [Michael] and both my grandfathers are from Ramallah. The seven family clans who originally inhabited Ramallah are all Christian. Today, there are more Ramallah people in the United States and other countries than in Ramallah. My six aunts and three uncles on my father's side along with their spouses, children, and grandchildren all live in Florida. Some I have met and others I have never met.

On my mother's side, from three aunts and four uncles, only six of their children remain in Ramallah; many of their children and grand-children have emigrated. My grandmother is from Lydda where the Tel Aviv airport now stands. All her relatives came to Ramallah as refugees in 1948. Some are still in Ramallah but others have had to move several times before they found a permanent refuge.

I have three sisters and one brother. My brother Hanna [John] and my older sister Joyce left Ramallah to study in the United States in the early 1950s. My brother was unable to come home. The State of Israel did not allow any Palestinians who were outside the country during a census taken immediately after the 1967 war to have residency rights, nor the right to return to their homeland. Nevertheless, from the diaspora, my brother devoted his life to the struggle of the Palestinian people. After leaving the United States, he lived in Jordan and then moved to Lebanon. Since 1976, now some thirty years, he has been among the disappeared. My oldest sister was not able to come back to visit for seventeen years. She left our home in Ramallah when I was a young girl of twelve years old, and when she saw me again, I was married with three children.

My younger sister married a man from Ramallah who immigrated with his family to the United States, and she left with him. My youngest sister had to go with her family to Jordan for economic reasons because her husband found work in Amman. They settled there. Eventually, my mother left her home in Ramallah because she was unable to get adequate health care and nursing services here. I am the only one left in Ramallah. For a time, I had my three children, their spouses, and grandchildren. But my sons also could not find work here. My youngest son could not attend college here when Birzeit University was closed. Only my daughter remains, and now her son and daughter have left for Jordan to go to college.

While there are sometimes signs of hope for those of us left behind, we constantly suffer not only the hard conditions of everyday life under occupation, but the isolation and deprivation that comes from having our families separated from us. And, of course, we worry about our own future and the future of our children.

Once I made the trip to the bridge and crossed into Jordan to be with my mother for two weeks. The only thing she asked me to carry with me this time from her home in Ramallah was a phrase of Arabic poetry that is framed in her bedroom. It reads, "I will have patience and persevere until patience knows that I am persevering in things that are even more bitter and thorny than patience itself." Patience in Arabic is *sabir*, the same name for the cactus plant whose thick leaves are full of bitter water and thorns.

More than half of the Palestinian population of Ramallah had to leave for many reasons—economic, educational, health and general well-being. Those who left are called by different names: refugees, internally displaced, asylum seekers, deportees, and economic migrants. We should remember, however, that all those who are compelled by severe political, economic, and social conditions to leave their land and culture, regardless of the labels given to them by others, are uprooted people. They have been forced to leave their land and culture because of persecution, war, violence, and the violation of human and community rights.

The deliberate displacement of the Palestinians by Israel as a matter of policy continues today through the confiscation and expropriation of our land, natural resources, and water; through the demolition of villages and houses; through the imposition of closures and embargoes on food and medicine; through restrictions on our movement; and through making it almost impossible to run a business or earn a living. Direct and structural violence directed at persons, communities, and the entire Palestinian population, are gradually destroying our social fabric, economic infrastructure, and natural environment. We experience permanent unemployment, increased marginalization, and exclusion.

Israel justifies these forms of violence in the name of "security" for a narrow ethnic and religiously-based Israeli nationalism. But surely security needs are mutual. For those uprooted from their communities, the loss of human dignity is an overpowering consequence of displacement. My uprooted family members speak about their many losses: of family, friends, and community; of familiar spiritual, religious, and cultural structures that nurture and define their basic human identity; of social status, property, employment, and economic resources. And, of course, security.

An Ecumenical Perspective

One of the best things that happened to me as a young woman was attending the Nairobi Assembly of the World Council of Churches in 1975 as a Quaker delegate. Never had I encountered such a wide range of Christians from so many parts of the world, involved in the struggles of the world. In the years after Nairobi, I became more and more involved in the work of the World Council of Churches, eventually serving on its Central Committee and on its commission on Dialogue with People of Living Faiths. All this gave me new insight into issues of religious difference, both among Christians and among people of other faiths.

My background as a Palestinian Christian inclined me naturally toward ecumenical work. Let me explain why. My two grandfathers were brothers. Their family name is Mikhail, a Christian name, and, with the rest of their brothers and sisters, they were members of the Orthodox Church. In the late eighteenth century, many missionary movements came to Palestine. As I have said, each church, for one reason or another, wanted a "presence" in the Holy Land. Most of them built new churches and served the people who joined their churches by, in many cases, building schools and hospitals.

The Society of Friends, called the Quakers, had a different interest. They did not build a church. The first thing they did was to start a school for girls in Ramallah at the request of our community. Many decades later, they built a meetinghouse and a boys school. When people applied to become members, thinking that they would benefit from a Friends education, they were most often refused. Quakers were not interested in gaining new members. They saw us all as Christians to start with and did not want simply to rearrange Christians into different denominations.

My grandfather on my mother's side lost his wife at a very early age, leaving him with four girls and four boys. He remarried soon after. He was a well-to-do man and decided to give more freedom to his children to compensate for the loss of their mother. My mother asked to go to the Friends School because that is where her friends were going. My aunts chose to go to St. Joseph's Catholic School and two of them joined the Order of St. Joseph and became nuns. My mother was eventually married under the care of the Society of Friends. Two of my four uncles joined the Anglican School in Jerusalem and, on marriage, shifted to the Anglican tradition. One remained Orthodox. The fourth married an American Baptist missionary and joined the Baptists. So, you see, my entire family is ecumenical—a large household that is an example of Christian diversity. But ours, like most grassroots diversity within Christianity, is not theological but situational. When we meet together, we have most things in common, even though our separate churches have given us different experiences.

My family is an example of most of the Christians in Palestine. I dare say that very few of us were converted from other faiths. Most of us were just rearranged. And in some cases, that rearrangement did lead to estrangement from one another. Our divisions have sometimes distorted the very message of Christ. Our challenge, as churches and as Christians, is to turn again to the one living God.

Over the years, I have also had the privilege of welcoming into my home in Ramallah people from many different churches and countries. I went out of my way as a Palestinian woman to share hospitality, and to offer my time and my understanding of our situation. At times it was exhausting. My children and husband used to tell me that I should put a sign on our front door: "Christian Information Center." And when I would take two aspirins after hours of painful dialogue, once again reviewing the history and hardships of our situation as Palestinians, my children would tease me that maybe I should have offered aspirin to my guests along with the tea and cookies. My children were wonderful for my humility and sense of perspective!

These personal encounters in my home were truly world expanding. But sometimes they were taxing, too. I recall one American guest who, after staying in our home, exclaimed with surprise how clean it was, implicitly revealing her expectation that a Palestinian home would not be clean. Another couple from Kansas who were sharing a meal in my home after 1967 and the beginning of the military occupation turned to me immediately after we said grace and asked, "How do you feel now after the Israelis liberated the rest of their homeland?" I nearly choked! I put on the best smile I could manage and said, "What? Which homeland? Whose homeland?" And they thought I had prepared that elaborate meal in celebration!

My late husband was the principal of the Friends Boys School in Ramallah during a very critical time from 1968 to 1986. In the early '80s there was a great deal of tension in the West Bank due to Israeli car-bomb attacks against three of our mayors. One bomb attack injured the legs of the mayor of Ramallah. The mayor of Nablus lost both of his legs due to another bombing. The mayor of Al-Bireh was late that day. When he heard of what happened to the others, he consequently asked soldiers to check his car and garage. The Israeli Druze soldier who dismantled the third bomb unfortunately lost his eyesight. There were widespread demonstrations, and a curfew was imposed.

One evening in the midst of all this tragedy, we received a phone call from an American Quaker; he was very concerned. An American teacher in the school had reported to him that some of our students had thrown stones at Israeli soldiers. He asked me, "How do we respond to our constituency? Why do students at the school use violence?" I answered him and said, "How should I respond to you as a Christian pacifist when you say nothing about the recent violence of Israelis or about the structural violence from which we are suffering on a daily basis?" And then I continued, "We need prophets of justice rather than the prophets of judgment!" It made me see how much the discourse about violence is controlled by the powerful. When our students throw stones, it is violence. When the Israeli soldiers brandish their weapons, it is law and order. When young Palestinians commit acts of desperate violence against the occupation, it is called terrorism. When Israelis commit acts of desperate and indefensible violence, it is called security.

Each Family's Tragedy

Finally, let me tell you a little more about my own family's tragedy. In 1976, my older and only brother, Hanna Mikhail, disappeared in the war in Lebanon and is still missing more than thirty years later. Hanna was a graduate of Haverford College and held a Ph.D. from Harvard University. He was a poet, a writer, and a political scientist. He lectured at Princeton and was an assistant professor at the University of Washington in Seattle. He was a member of the international Russell Tribunal. When the 1967 war left us in a newly occupied West Bank, however, Hanna wanted to return home to be with his people. But he was denied entry to Palestine, his own home, because he was not counted by Israel as one of the residents of the occupied lands immediately following the war. Meanwhile, any Jewish person from any part of the world could live and settle in Palestine according to the law of the "right of return." But Hanna, who had been born and raised here, had no right to return.

With no possibility of returning home Hanna abandoned his secure future as a scholar and adopted the uncertainties and dangers of being a volunteer in the Palestinian Liberation Organization (PLO) as part of his people's struggle for their rights and freedom. His simplicity of life, his idealism, and his commitment to struggle for self-determination was admired by all. The young people called him a prophet. One wrote that he "represented the best of the once free-wheeling Palestinian revolution."[1] Later, with the beginning of the Lebanese War in 1976, he became among the disappeared. I agonized with my parents about the uncertainty of my brother's situation. I appealed to many organizations to help; I tried to explore all options and to knock on all doors to see if we could find out where he was or what had happened to him.

At this time, we had a houseguest, a notable American pacifist, whom I thought would help me apply to Amnesty International to seek information. He exclaimed: "Your brother worked with the PLO, a terrorist organization, and it is against my principles to do anything for people who choose the path of violence." The self-righteous detachment of this so-called pacifist distressed me so profoundly at the time that I knew I had to reexamine my whole understanding of the vocation of being a peacemaker. In one act of judgment, my brother had been labeled and classified and then had lost his basic rights as a human being. This man did not seem to understand the utter cruelty of his judgmental attitude. He did not seem to comprehend that my brother was never allowed to come back to his home and his parents, because he was out of the country during the 1967 war, while any Jew under the "right of return" law could come and live in our land. He did not seem to think that the dispossession of Palestinians, the confiscation of our land, and the subsequent occupation of our land was itself a form of violence.

I wished only to locate my brother and to know if his basic human rights were being met. Alas, I was told that my brother was connected to the PLO—a so-called violent terrorist organization. That seemed to be all anyone needed to know. So it was with many in the pacifist churches. Rather than being helpful, they were judgmental. Did they worry about my brother's basic right to life, to liberty, and to security? Apparently not. Did they insist that my brother should not be subjected to torture or to cruel, inhuman, and degrading treatment no matter what his affiliation? Apparently not.

The famous scholar Edward Said described my brother, Hanna Mikhail, as a man who lived and died retaining his "Quaker modesty and plainness." Said added that "He believed in human liberation, decent co-existence between Arabs and Jews, social and economic justice for men and women." Said goes on to describe my brother Hanna as a distinguished role model, a man who did not debase himself or his people. Why? Because he lived his ideals and died for them.[2]

Let this personal and painful story about my brother not distract us from the wider tragedy. There is not one of today's nine million Palestinians, many of whom live somewhere in forced exile, who has not felt the pain of personal tragedy. There are so many stories. Each one is overwhelming for someone. But every story must become part of an ocean of truth that will help the world understand what is happening in my part of the Middle East.

A Japanese poet once wrote: "The world grows stronger as each story is told." And yet, most of the world ignores these stories, the stories of countless people, and instead records the history of wars and ideas. The day's top stories from the authoritative voice of the television newscaster on CNN never include the simple stories of hundreds of Palestinians waiting collectively thousands of hours just to cross the bridge to Amman, or the stories of the families of who have been dispossessed of their land, or the stories of the families who wait in anguish for the imprisoned or disappeared. We want the truth to be simple, but every time we insist on such a simplistic portrayal we diminish truth and deprive ourselves of the richness of each human story.

2

AL NAKBA, THE CATASTROPHE

IN 1998, I was asked by peace and justice groups in Sweden to speak at a gathering in the Public Square in Stockholm.[1] In that year, people all over the world were observing the fiftieth anniversary of the UN Declaration on Human Rights. And in that year, the State of Israel was also observing its fiftieth anniversary. I was asked as a Palestinian to offer my perspective. For those of us who are Palestinians, we had lived through fifty years of dispossession and continual betrayal by Israel. And we had also lived through fifty years of the inability of the United Nations and its member states to enforce its countless resolutions in support of the Palestinian people. It was not a moment for celebration, but a time for the sober recollection of the events that have shaped our recent history. In Palestine, we call those events of 1948, now sixty years ago, *Al Nakba*, "The Catastrophe," as hundreds of thousands of Palestinians were dispossessed of their homes, agricultural fields, and property, and many were forced to become refugees in their own land.

Karl Marx observed that when history appears to repeat itself, it comes around "the first time as tragedy, the second time as farce." Tragedy, we know. Farce is defined as an absurd and useless comic drama in which authority, order, and morality become a sham. There has not been much room for comedy in the way history has repeated itself in the

Arab world, including Palestine; rather, tragedy follows upon tragedy. *Al Nakba* was followed by another *nakba,* the absurd and useless drama of the Israeli government that has increasingly controlled every aspect of our daily lives, causing incalculable physical, mental, and spiritual hardship.

On November 29, 1947, the UN General Assembly passed Resolution 181 calling for the partition of Palestine into separate Jewish and Arab states. As is now well known, David Ben-Gurion, the first Israeli prime minister, accepted the Partition Plan tactically, as part of his strategy to gain all of Palestine. What he really accepted was the establishment of a Jewish state, but he did not accept the idea of Palestine, of borders, and of Jerusalem as *corpus seperatum,* a city that would be under direct international administration.

The 1947 Partition Plan was never implemented. On May 14, 1948, the Jewish People's Council led by Ben-Gurion met at the Tel Aviv museum and issued its declaration of the establishment of the State of Israel. The declaration was carefully worded so as to draw on Resolution 181 as a legitimizing document for the creation of the Jewish state but it gave no mention of partition, borders, or the other elements of the resolution.

The Declaration read: "On the 29th November, 1947 the United Nations General Assembly passed a resolution calling for the establishment of a Jewish State in Eretz-Israel. The General Assembly required the inhabitants of Eretz-Israel to take such steps as were necessary on their part for the implementation of this resolution. The recognition by the United Nations of the right of the Jewish people to establish their State is irrevocable" (Israel Ministry of Foreign Affairs). The Jewish People's Council saw that the necessary steps were:

1. To establish themselves on the land of Palestine;

2. To reduce and remove significantly the majority of Palestinian Arabs from Palestine; and

3. To ensure the absorption of dispersed Palestinians in the Arab world and elsewhere so as to eliminate Palestinian claims to Palestine.

The human cost of this plan was and still is very high. More than 200,000 Palestinians were dispossessed of their properties and dispersed between 1947 and 1948, and in the 1948 Arab-Israeli War another 550,000 to 600,000 were dispossessed of their properties and over four hundred Palestinian villages were completely depopulated or destroyed. By the end of the 1948 war, Israel was in full control of 77 percent of Palestine from which some 800,000 Palestinians became refugees. The total Palestinian population then was estimated to be 1.4 million. In the conquered 77 percent—which is 20 percent more than was allotted to the Jewish state by the Partition Plan—150,000 Palestinians remained who ultimately became citizens of Israel, but second-class citizens. Now they number over one million people, some 20 percent of the Israeli population.

In the wake of the Six-Day War of 1967, in June of that year, Israel occupied the remaining 22 percent of Palestine, Gaza, the West Bank, and East Jerusalem as well as the Syrian Golan Heights and the Egyptian Sinai. In 1967, the West Bank and Gaza had a population of just over one million; now it is approximately 3.5 million. To this day, sixty years after *Al Nakba*, relief workers are still trying to organize services for Palestinian refugees who were uprooted more than once, dispossessed, denied the right of return, and denied compensation for their property.

The majority of Palestinian refugees live in Jordan, Syria, Lebanon, and the Occupied Territories in the most difficult situations, but still demand their right of return to their towns and villages. A fourth generation has been born in these camps and if you ask a child about his or her identity, that child might say, "I am a Palestinian from Jaffa or from Haifa or from Jerusalem." This may seem to be an unusual way of establishing connection and taking pride in one's background and identity. But the sense of identity that the dispossessed feel for the places they have only heard of, but never seen, can be very strong.

Future generations may look back at these serial tragedies one after the other and see them differently, but those of us who have lived through the past decades of despair, empty promises, shattered dreams, loss of land, water, and resources and denial of basic human rights find it often difficult to keep faith in the struggle against seemingly overwhelming odds. I believe that what we call the Catastrophe will be, for future generations, the critical issue that deserved the sustained attention of the world and yet did not get it. It continues to have political implications for the whole world and emotional resonance for people far beyond Palestine. It is our fear that this untreated Catastrophe will be a future Catastrophe for many other people.

As a Palestinian Christian, I am a founding member of Sabeel, an ecumenical, grassroots, liberation-theology movement that works for justice, peace, and reconciliation in Israel and Palestine. Most liberation theologians begin with the exodus, the great drama in which a people in slavery and bondage to another were freed. Of course, there is much about the drama of the exodus that is difficult. In undertaking to rescue the Israelites from their bondage, God assures them that God will lead them into a "land flowing with milk and honey." But in addition to the milk and honey, the land had an abundance of people—Hittites, Amorites, Canaanites. The Israelites are told to drive them out and "not let anything that breathes remain alive" (Deuteronomy 20).

To me, this mandate for genocide is utterly contrary to my understanding of God and I reject it. Does God promise land to one people at the expense of others, and then give a divine mandate to cleanse the land of its inhabitants? Any literalist reading of this frightens me, not just as a Palestinian, but as a human being. But the problem ceases to be a solely theological problem and takes on immediate relevance when Jewish settlers come to our land today and claim that God promised it to them in the Bible.

There is a beautiful arch at the entry to Sabeel's building in Jerusalem on which a verse is written in Arabic: "You shall know the truth and the truth shall set you free" (John 8:32). Speaking the truth is not always easy. What is the truth of Bible? What is God trying to say to us through the prophets and poets? What is God trying to make clear to us through Jesus? I interpret the Bible—for me both the Old and New Testaments—in the light of the resounding themes of justice and compassion. God is a God of justice and compassion, not of war and vengeance and exclusivity. The truth of Scripture is not about literal words, things, and concepts. The truth of Scripture is about relationship—between God and us, and between us as persons. When Jesus said, "I am the way, the truth, and the life," he proclaimed that truth comes to us not as a dogma, but as a life—a life of love, justice, and action.

Truth must be put into practice. If what we know is abstract, impersonal, apart from us, it cannot be truth. For truth involves a vulnerable and faithful risk taking. It involves real relationship. Half-truths fill government halls, institutions, and the media. To speak the truth about our Catastrophe may well be dangerous. I might suffer, be harassed, or even go to prison for standing up for truth. But I will never kill for truth, for truth is incompatible with violence. I yearn to live truth with love, so that our bewildered hearts come home and are able to dwell in a world in which truth tellers are the freedom fighters, struggling for abundant life for all God's people.

Palestine and Palestinians remain, despite Israel's concerted efforts to get rid of us or to make us ineffective. Palestine and its people have not disappeared. The more Israel wraps itself in exclusivity, the more it assists us to stay on and fight the injustices. In this context, I have to speak the truth. I have to speak what is true. It is true, for example, that we are losing day by day more of our land, due to Israeli settlements and bypass roads. We are forced to stand by while we see fields bulldozed, plants, crops, and olive trees uprooted, and homes demolished. It is true that Palestinians from the West Bank are not allowed to enter Jerusalem. Israel has succeeded in its continuous effort to Judaize the city, spreading unchecked Israeli power, changing the character of Jerusalem, and even depriving its Palestinian inhabitants of their land and identity cards while bulldozing many homes. It is true that there is now no connection between Gaza and the West Bank for Palestinians, making normal traffic between us impossible. Practically speaking, I cannot go to Gaza, Jerusalem, or Israel, but anyone from the audiences I address in Sweden, Canada, or the United States can. It is true, practically speaking, that none of those fourth-generation refugees in the camps can return to Jaffa, Haifa, or Jerusalem even for a visit, but any young Jewish student of the same age from anywhere in the world can go to these places and speak of it as a "birthright."

If it hopes for peace and security, the Israeli government cannot bottle up and contain 3.5 million occupied Palestinians without any rights to self-determination and sovereignty. The motto of the Oslo process was

"Land for Peace." Following Oslo, it became very obvious that it was "Land for People." Israel has been taking the land under the guise of safeguarding its own security and giving the Palestinian National Authority only the right to take care of the Palestinian people without true sovereignty, without financial assistance, and without an end to occupation. The years since Oslo have not resulted in a process for peace, but have led to agreements that are creating increasingly volatile conditions on the ground. Following the failure of Oslo, the "road map" was agreed upon under pressure to start negotiations for a Palestinian state. It, too, has failed to bring about progress. Palestinians want peace and strive for peace, but in the absence of meaningful peaceful channels for legitimate change, many will feel an increased need for resistance.

Despite the clear reality that things are getting worse for Palestinians, year after year, I want to testify to the resilience and continued power of the Palestinian cause, which has continued to move people's minds and hearts in many parts of the world. In Israel, too, there are some strong voices for justice and human rights for the Palestinians. Most people can readily see that international law and UN resolutions should apply equally to all. The philosopher I. F. Stone asked long ago, in a 1979 article, "How can we talk of human rights and ignore them for the Palestinian Arabs? How can Israel talk of the Jewish right to a homeland and deny one to the Palestinians? How can there be peace without a measure of justice?"[2] He believed that a binational state "is the path to reconciliation, and reconciliation alone can guarantee Israel's survival. Israel can exhaust itself in new wars. It can commit suicide. It can pull down the pillars on itself and its neighbors."

Stone went on to say, "But it can live only by reviving the spirit of fraternity and justice and conciliation that the prophets preached and the other Zionism sought to apply." Here, he refers to the "other Zionism," the binationalists and those who favored true equality for Palestinian Arabs. Stone felt that either two equal states in Palestine must emerge or a binational one. As it seems now, because of its own policies, Israel is missing the opportunity to resolve the problem with a two-state solution, and has now created conditions on the ground that can be resolved only by a democratic binational state. It has created the conditions on the ground—a fragmented Swiss cheese of land filled with spaces of Israeli settlement linked with Israel-only highways—that make a viable Palestinian state almost impossible. The wall in process of construction makes quite clear that Israel intends to keep these impossible, unilaterally set "boundaries."

Israel and its partners need to face up to reality. The Palestinians will not continue to live under Israel's rule indefinitely. Today, the occupied Palestinian territories are a ticking time bomb. Either Israel stops the expansion of settlements and moves rapidly into negotiations that implement UN resolutions, apply international humanitarian law, and end the occupation, or Israel will face a new cycle of resistance. Resistance is simply the natural reaction to Israel's unnatural occupation. There should be no surprise in Israel or elsewhere in the world when the next wave of Palestinian resistance explodes. There should be nothing surprising about the refusal of another generation to inherit pain and powerlessness, or another generation to resist the catastrophic subjugation and oppression. If Israel wishes to continue to impose an apartheid-like system on Palestinians, then is should be dealt with as an apartheid state.

It is my hope that the suffering of war and the catastrophe of *Al Nakba* will be replaced by a new era of peace and justice for all Palestinians and Israelis. It is my hope that all of us, in the face of human suffering, will be strong enough and courageous enough to speak the truth and reject the violence of silence. This is our challenge—to speak the truth and break the silence!

3

HUMAN RIGHTS

Ah, you who make iniquitous decrees, who write oppressive statutes, to turn aside the needy from justice and to rob the poor of my people of their right, that widows may be your spoil, and that you may make the orphans your prey!—Isa. 10:1-2

Recognition of the inherent dignity and the equal and inalienable rights of all members of the human family is the foundation of freedom, justice and peace in the world.—Introduction, Universal Declaration of Human Rights

I AM NOT A HUMAN RIGHTS EXPERT. However, I have learned through the years that you do not need to be an expert in human rights to know that you are being oppressed. I make no pretense to being qualified to speak on the many aspects of international law and human rights. But I know from experience how very hard things are in Palestine, now sixty years after the events of 1948: the expansion of Jewish settlements in the occupied Palestinian territories, the construction of a wall aimed at unilaterally annexing more of our land, the continued military occupation of the West Bank, Gaza, and East Jerusalem. All the while, international law and UN resolutions sit collecting dust. The political landscape changes with elections in both Israel and Palestine. Global powers maneuver a response to the electoral success of Hamas.

And humanitarian aid from wealthy countries is withheld and used as a carrot in an attempt to change the positions of Palestinian political elites without regard to the reality of ordinary families struggling to secure their daily bread and access to basic medical services. Sixty percent of Palestinians now live below the poverty line.[1]

Since the establishment of the State of Israel and the adoption of the Universal Declaration of Human Rights in 1948, we have seen the systematic violation of Palestinian national and individual rights. In theory, both international human rights conventions and international humanitarian law guarantee the rights of Palestinians, chiefly through the Fourth Geneva Convention. Furthermore, UN resolutions were to resolve the refugee crisis and end the military occupation. Obviously, in practice, the situation has been dramatically different. The failure of the international community to uphold human rights, humanitarian laws, and to implement relevant UN resolutions has resulted in our continued dispossession and oppression rather than our independence and freedom.

Since the 1948 *Nakba*, Arabs and Palestinians have sought the support of the United Nations to protect our rights. But as any one can clearly see, Palestinian refugees are still in refugee camps, now in their fourth generation. The Catastrophe of expropriation and dispossession did not end in 1948, but keeps on happening. Even now, Palestinian land is continuously and illegally expropriated for the exclusive use and benefit of Israeli Jews. This includes the confiscation of Palestinian lands for the expansion of Jewish settlements, the confiscation of Palestinian land for building bypass roads and highways that connect the settlements to one another, and the confiscation of Palestinian lands, including ancient olive groves, for building the apartheid wall. The denial of basic human rights continues unchecked by the international community and its human rights protection mechanisms.

The right to home and residence is, for us, so basic, yet remains under threat. In my own family, as I have said, my brother was denied permission to return to his home and loved ones. At about the same time, my brother-in-law was mayor of our city, Ramallah. He was deported in 1968 by the Israelis. My husband tried in vain to convince his church leader to help him secure a permit to see his brother and to arrange for his wife and children to join him. He was unsuccessful. Later, we tried once again to see if the bishop could secure a permit for my brother-in-law simply to attend his mother's funeral in 1974, but it was impossible.

I mention both these cases, not because they are my family members or because they are in any way unique in the Palestinian experience. Rather, they represent the experience of almost everyone in Palestine. We all know people and have loved ones who have been deported from their cities and towns or who have been "denied entry," thus preventing them from returning to their homes. According to the Palestinian Diaspora and Refugee Center, since 1967, some 150,000 Palestinians have had their residency rights taken away from them by the Israeli Ministry of Interior.[2] And I mention my brother and brother-in-law because I know from experience that there is no place of appeal—not the government that has instituted these practices, nor the churches that make ineffective efforts to respond to appeals for help. And yet the right to be treated humanely, even if one is a political prisoner, even if one is a member of the PLO, is a human right. And the right to affirm a nationality and to self-determination is a human right. It is in the very nature of human rights that they cannot be applied to some and denied to others.

The United Nations and Palestinian Rights

Though Palestinian rights are not confined to East Jerusalem, the West Bank, and the Gaza Strip, let me focus first on Israeli practices in these areas, simply for the reason that most of the UN resolutions regarding Palestinians relate to these areas, the occupied Palestinian territories. These are the territories occupied by Israel in 1967 and claimed as the State of Palestine by the PLO in the Palestinian Declaration of Independence of 1988. In 2004, the UN Development Program *Arab Human Development Report* noted once again that the United Nations "condemned Israel's occupation of Palestine as a crime against humanity and a flagrant violation of human rights."[3]

Many scholars view the Universal Declaration of Human Rights as part and parcel of international law, thus making it a duty for states to respect its provisions, including those states that are militarily occupying other people. In practice, this means that we, the Palestinians, should have the protection provided for by UN Conventions. As human beings, we should have the protection of human rights law. Therefore, under military occupation, Palestinian civilians should have the status of protected persons. This is not the case, however. The reality is that we have the protection of no one.

Israel is continuing its violation of our rights, including the targeting of civilians, extrajudicial killings, and even torture during interrogation, despite the 1999 High Court ruling against it. The denial of the right to freedom of movement, denial of the right of return to one's own country, and denial of family rights, including family unification and reunification, constitute another set of human rights violations. Despite Israel's gross violation of our rights and our human dignity nothing has changed. But it seems that either international law and the community of states are not in a position to stop this human tragedy, or there is no willingness to do so. While the whole international community, except Israel, recognizes that we are victims of ongoing violations, no significant pressure, such as economic sanctions, has yet been applied to the culprit.

Today there are some ten thousand Palestinian political prisoners in Israeli jails. Approximately, 750 to one thousand are under administrative detention and are held without charge or trial. Of these, the Israeli human rights organization B'Tselem estimates that some three hundred are minors. At least eight thousand homes in the occupied Palestinian territories have been demolished since the beginning of the occupation, leaving tens of thousands without shelter. Israeli colonial settlements and outposts have mushroomed to over two hundred in the West Bank with a population of over four hundred thousand, including East Jerusalem. In order to connect these illegal colonies, particularly in the West Bank, some 350 kilometers of highway and bypass roads have been built on confiscated land for the exclusive use of Israelis. All of these acts are illegal under international law, namely the Fourth Geneva Convention.

I am tempted to ask, "Why is it so?" Are we seen as humanly unequal in our rights and aspirations? Or, is international law—an expression of the norms developed and accepted by civilized nations—so weak that it cannot provide us with shelter against Israel's illegal policies and human rights violations? Or, is it that the weakness comes from the fact that Palestine's occupier is granted a special status?

We in the occupied Palestinian territories, as protected persons, are entitled to respect for our persons, our dignity, our family rights, religious convictions and practices, cultures and customs. We should be protected against all acts of violence. We still have no territorial sovereignty. Most of our land is being annexed to Israel, and the transfer of the Israeli population into the occupied Palestinian territory, which is illegal according to international law, continues.

The Fragmentation of the West Bank

Military conquest cannot justify permanent territorial claims. This is the cornerstone of the international legal order. The United Nations and the European Union have consistently confirmed the illegality of the Israeli occupation and the building of settlements on occupied land. But during the so-called "peace process" following the Oslo Accords in 1993, land confiscation was actually accelerated. Existing settlements were expanded and new ones continue to be built even now. Before 1991, 45 percent of the West Bank was in the hands of Israelis. Now, according to respected human rights organizations, Israel controls 67 percent of the land—land that is now inaccessible to the Palestinians. The question of settlements is at the heart of the peace process. Again, the words of the Hebrew prophet Isaiah are appropriate for today: "Ah, you who join house to house, who add field to field, until there is room for no one but you, and you are left to live alone in the midst of the land!" (Isa. 5:8).

We call this increased fragmentation of Palestinian land the "bantustanization" of the occupied Palestinian territories of the West Bank and Gaza, or the "new apartheid" in Palestine. You might ask about the Palestinian Authority, saying, "Didn't the Oslo Accords place you under your own rule? Isn't your situation any better?" On the contrary, the

Oslo Accords have triggered an Israeli policy that can best be described as the creation of "bantustans" in the Occupied Territories. I live in the bantustan of Ramallah. Others live in the bantustan of Bethlehem, the bantustan of Jericho, the bantustan of Hebron, and so on. Much of the world has yet to acknowledge the term *apartheid*, in describing the Palestinian situation, but in fact this is the reality. The policy of the Accords has been a policy of "apartness" or "separation." It is not just the separation of Palestinians and Israelis, but also the separation of Palestinians from any effective interaction with one another. Israel's silent, but steady, gain in control over the West Bank makes the territorial integrity of a viable independent Palestinian state more unlikely every day. Meanwhile, Gaza, despite Israeli withdrawal to the borders, still lies victim to military incursions and remains under military occupation with Israel controlling the border, air, and sea.

Perhaps the most dangerous reality on the ground at this time is the apartheid wall. It is designed, ultimately, to be 450 miles long and brazenly defies any of the current peace plans, including the "road map," while disregarding any rights-based framework to resolving the conflict. The International Court of Justice ruled on July 9, 2004, that the wall stood contrary to international law and placed Israel under obligation to dismantle it and furthermore to make reparation for damage caused by its construction. Israel has yet to do so. Over a quarter-million Palestinians will be directly affected by this wall.

The wall is built on Palestinian land. At places, it makes deep cuts into the 1967 Palestinian territories. Land has been confiscated, buildings and orchards destroyed in order to build it. At the time I write this, 102,350 trees have been uprooted in the construction of the wall, and this is continuing. When it is completed, thousands of Palestinians will be trapped in the no-man's land between the wall and the State of Israel, cutting them off from the rest of Palestinian society and from their agricultural land. The special UN report on the wall noted that "The land between the Barrier and the Green Line constitutes some of the most fertile in the West Bank. It is currently the home for 49,400 West Bank Palestinians living in 38 villages and towns."[4]

Another striking element of Israeli policy is the demolition of Palestinian homes. This is a policy used since the occupation in 1967, but it has continued and intensified to this day. One official reason for demolishing the homes is that no building permits have been given. It should be noted that it is extremely difficult, if not impossible, for Palestinians to get building permits. Moreover, the demolished houses are often located near Israeli installations, settlements, or bypass roads and are effectively demolished in order to expand the infrastructure of Israel's occupation. The Fourth Geneva Convention calls the wanton destruction of houses and civilian property a "war crime," and all human rights organizations have documented and condemned the practice. Since the beginning of the occupation, however, more than eighteen thousand homes have been demolished. In Gaza, more than twenty-four thousand people have been rendered homeless this way. In the single month of May 2004, in the town of Rafah, four thousand Palestinians were made homeless after the Israeli army destroyed their homes. Where are the thousands of people who lived in the demolished houses to live? What about the rights of these families to housing and property? Was the demolished house that of an activist in the resistance? How, then, do you justify collective punishment against a spouse, children, a family? But the news media rarely notes the violence of house demolitions anymore. It is not new, but routine.

Water is another critical issue. The settlers, ten times fewer in number than the Palestinians, account for twice as much land and twice as much water use. Israelis and the Palestinians are supposed to share water resources, but the "sharing" is vastly unequal. Israeli citizens have almost unlimited water use, while Palestinians have severe water shortages, especially in the summer. Domestic use on the West Bank is sixty liters per person per day, while Israeli use is more than four-and-a-half times that at 280 liters per person per day. Health, sanitation, crops, and the economy are all compromised by overt discrimination in water use. Our water is siphoned off for Israeli settlements and gardens and then sold back to us. Moreover, in the middle of a regional water crisis, the occupation army has destroyed some thirty-five thousand meters of water pipes in the process of constructing the wall.

Looking to the Future

The closure of East Jerusalem enforced by the Israeli authorities since March 30, 1993, reinforces the isolation of the city from the remainder of the Occupied Territories and divides the West Bank into two entities. Jerusalem was always the center of Palestine and it connected the north and the south. Now, it is very difficult to travel between the north and south of the West Bank without going through East Jerusalem. From my home in Ramallah, I could previously reach Bethlehem in a little more than a half-hour; for Jericho, it was about a thirty-five-minute trip. Now that is impossible. It is a journey of three to five hours, depending upon the checkpoints.

The closure of Jerusalem and Israel to West Bank and Gaza Palestinians, the lack of connection between Gaza and the West Bank, the restriction of movement between the north and south of the West Bank—all of these things make it difficult to move anywhere. In human rights terms, this is not simply about the restriction of movement. It is about the policy of fragmenting a community and the effect this ultimately has on the right to health, education, and basic well-being. This fragmentation takes an enormous human and economic toll. As of July 2007, the number of checkpoints dividing Palestinian territories into enclaves is 539, a type of forced fragmentation that has precipitated a large-scale humanitarian crisis and adversely affected Palestinian economic and social rights.[5] According to the UN Office for Coordination of Humanitarian Affairs, "More than 38% of the West Bank is now taken by Israeli infrastructure."[6]

The policies of settlement expansion and increasing land confiscation measures are aimed at Judaizing Jerusalem and creating "facts on the ground" that violate international law and human rights. But this is not a plan for lasting peace. Peace cannot be achieved unless it is based on freedom, justice, and the removal of oppression inflicted on the Palestinian people. Our internationally recognized rights, as affirmed in relevant UN Security Council resolutions, need to be realized. These resolutions call for the end of occupation, condemn the illegal annexation of Jerusalem, and affirm the illegality of Jewish settlements in the occupied Palestinian territories. Israel is not above the law and measures should be taken against these policies. The only agreements that are capable of bringing about a permanent peace are those that guarantee an end to occupation and realize justice for Palestine, together with guaranteeing the right of return as well as compensation for Palestinian refugees.

It is difficult and painful for me, for my children and grandchildren, and for my people to continue to live with all of these violations of individual and community rights. I always ask myself, "When will that day come when we as Palestinians, as non-Jews, are treated without discrimination, with equality, in spite of our differences? Will we be allowed to have self-determination and sovereignty over our natural resources, land, and water? Will I experience again in my lifetime freedom of movement in my homeland?"

It is only a matter of time before the population between the Mediterranean and the Jordan River will be half Jewish Israeli and half Palestinian Arab. Now the Jewish Israelis are free and we are not. We are not equal by any scale of measurement. But the well-being of our two peoples is inextricably interrelated. Peace and respect for Palestinian human rights is not only for the sake of Palestinians. It is essential for the sake of the Israelis as well, and for the wider region. It is essential for the future peace and stability of the Middle East and the world.

The endless battering of Palestinians on a daily basis virtually imprisons us in our houses half of the time and the rest of the time within fragmented communities separated from each other by walls, ditches, and checkpoints, making the means of daily life, jobs, education, hospitals, all but inaccessible. This is done as a matter of policy, making life so intolerable that as many of us as possible will leave the country.

But despite the current Israeli government's intention, no degree of violence can succeed in subjugating the will of a people or destroying their spirit when they are struggling for their freedom, dignity and right to sovereignty on their own land. All Israeli attempts at intensifying the brutality of the occupation against the Palestinians have only led to the escalation of the conflict and increased our determination to gain our liberty. Conflicts can only be resolved politically and legally, on the basis of parity of rights and the global rule of law. I do hope that the Israeli public and the international community will realize the extreme danger of their policies before it is too late and more innocent blood is shed. And I hope the U.S. government will realize that its blind support and military aid to Israel is not necessarily to the long-term advantage of Israel or even in the best interest of the United States.

Our common future as Israelis and Palestinians makes it inevitable for us to try to heal the traumas of the past, right the wrongs of today, and build a better future for all. We should envision a future in which we apply a universal morality, emanating from our common God, measured by a simple standard of behavior, and valid for all people in all lands. These are the universal standards expressed in the Universal Declaration of Human Rights, and we must renew our common commitment to live up to them.

4

JERUSALEM: *AL-QUDS*, THE HOLY

"If you, even you, had only recognized on this day the things that make for peace! But now they are hidden from your eyes."
—*Luke 19:42*

I WAS BORN AND HAVE LIVED all my life in Ramallah, Palestine—one of the beautiful summer resorts in the Jerusalem mountain range. It is only fifteen kilometers north of Jerusalem. From the roof of my home, I can look south and see Jerusalem glittering like a ball of crystal in the night. I agonize that I am not allowed to go there. Jerusalem has always been for us the center, the heart that pumped life into all of Palestine. For many years, we have traveled to Jerusalem to go to Bethlehem, Hebron, Jericho, and Gaza. But without Jerusalem, Palestine is disjointed.

All my children and seven grandchildren were born in Jerusalem. Over the years, we have been treated in its hospitals. We have gone there for worship, cultural activities, visits to our family members, for work, and for getting visas to travel. Jerusalem is in the heart of every Palestinian. You see it in pictures, carvings, paintings, and posters in our homes, schools, public buildings, taxis, and buses. You hear the beautiful songs about it. Jerusalem is called the flower of all cities. In Arabic, Jerusalem is called *Al-Quds*—the sacred, the holy, the pure. As you walk in its Old

City, you can smell the aroma of incense and of so many spices. You see all kinds of candles and handicrafts. You are surrounded by a Christian and Muslim heritage of artistic and architectural achievement, which provides a testimony to the power of faith embodied in art and architecture. You hear the bells of the churches joined by the muezzins, the call to prayer, from minarets within the city.

For me, Jerusalem stands for freedom of mind, diversity, and universality. God is not exclusive; rather, God is within the reach of every person. In Jerusalem, I learned that the dignity of the individual is more important than all the protocols and rituals, and that our actions should be motivated by love rather than by the law. Prophets, mystics, and priests may point the ways to faith, and we may choose to follow whom we will.

The First Christians

Jerusalem speaks to our history as Middle Eastern Christians. With the establishment of the first community of Christians in Jerusalem, which dates back to apostolic times, the first Christian Church was established (Acts 2:4). It was from Jerusalem that Christianity spread to various parts of the Middle East and the rest of the world. By the fifth century, some of the Arab kingdoms in Syria, Jordan, Iraq, and Palestine had adopted Christianity.

Jerusalem's place in Christianity is illustrated by the symbolic medieval maps that show Jerusalem at the center of the universe, with the continents spreading out from Jerusalem like petals of a flower. While Jerusalem is sacred for Jews and Muslims alike, for those of us who are Christians, Jerusalem is the place where so much of the life of Jesus literally "takes place." In the Gospel of Luke, the drama of the life of Jesus is oriented toward Jerusalem. As Luke writes, "When the days drew near for him to be taken up, he set his face to go to Jerusalem" (9:51) in order to fulfill "everything that is written about the Son of Man" (18:31) "because it is impossible for a prophet to be killed outside of Jerusalem" (13:33). The great drama of Jesus' life, death, and resurrection is a Jerusalem drama. Jesus preached in the Temple in Jerusalem, overturned the tables of the merchants who had set up shop in the Temple, and celebrated a Passover supper with his disciples. He prayed in agony in the Garden of Gethsemane, carried his cross along the Via Dolorosa, and was crucified on Golgotha, the place called Calvary. It was in Jerusalem that Mary and the disciples saw Jesus with their own eyes, witnessing his resurrection and his ascension into heaven. Fifty days after his resurrection, the Holy Spirit poured out upon the disciples in Jerusalem and set them on fire, speaking in all the languages of the earth about the mighty events they had seen.

Among Western Christians, the celebration of Christmas assumes the greatest importance, but among Middle Eastern Christians it is the resurrection at Easter that has become the greatest celebration. For Palestinians, the experience of Golgotha is not a distant past or a sad memory; it is part of everyday indignity and oppression. Our Via Dolorosa is not a mere ritualistic procession through the narrow streets of the Old City of Jerusalem, but the fate of being subjugated and humiliated in our own land today. The mystery of resurrection holds for us a message of hope and unity and the ability of the oppressed to triumph. It gives us a message of life, confronting and overcoming death. This image has special meaning for people living under occupation.

Since the time of Jesus and after the resurrection, Jerusalem has been considered the "Mother of all Churches." In the Gospel of Matthew this image is evoked in the lament, "Jerusalem, Jerusalem, the city that kills the prophets and stones those who are sent to it! How often have I desired to gather your children together as a hen gathers her brood under her wings, and you were not willing!" (Matt. 23:37). Jesus' own yearning for a more peaceful Jerusalem is one that is echoed through the ages. As a Christian, I see the struggle of so many denominations over every inch of the Holy City, and I see all the local and international arguments about proprietary rights over this or that sacred place. Perhaps it is an expression of the desire to be close to the Holy City.

Today in Jerusalem there are hundreds of Christian churches. Judging by the abundance of Christian churches, monuments, and ruins, the number of Christian organizations and the presence of their representatives, you would think that Jerusalem would be the most Christian city in the world. Unfortunately, about a million pilgrims travel to the Holy Land every year without really being involved in the Passion of Christ. And for most, Palestinian Christians are invisible, unknown, or forgotten.

The contribution of Palestinian Christians to Palestine and the welfare of its people has always extended beyond our numbers. In architecture, business, education, medical services, law, and politics, Palestinian Christians have achieved much. Indeed, our contribution may explain the intensity of Israeli pressure on the Christian community, because of our constant emphasis on justice and pluralism. The Palestinian Christians of the Holy Land—all of them from the shopkeeper to the political leader—want to continue living where they are: in Jerusalem and in Palestine. They do not wish to leave. Their claim is historic and their achievements and contributions to the community as a whole are clear.

Palestinian Christians are referred to as the Palestinian embroidery—an interwoven and an integral part of the whole population. Because we refuse to separate ourselves from our Muslim brothers and sisters and because we remain loyal to our national identity, the rest of the world has no idea how to handle Palestinian Christians. Although we are really the modern heirs of the disciples of Jesus in Jerusalem, we have become unknown, unacknowledged, and forgotten. Despite all of this, we are a community that has maintained a strong witness to the gospel in the land of the incarnation and resurrection. Ours is a highly educated community, with deep historical roots. It is, unfortunately, a community that is diminishing every day as a result of the political, economic, and religious pressures of the Israeli occupation.

Along with our Muslim Palestinian brothers and sisters, we believe that Palestinian Christianity is worth saving. We cannot comprehend why the Israeli government treats us as a threat. During the millennium celebrations in 2000, there was much made of the second millennium of the Christian movement, but this was also a moment in which we began to see more clearly the dying remnant of Palestinian Christians. For us, we tried to see this as an occasion to consider how to strengthen Palestinian Christians and support them, so that we might stay, survive, and attain our basic human rights, so that we might be empowered and transformed to continue our witness in our land, the land of Jesus the Liberator.

The Annexation of Jerusalem

For Palestinians, Jerusalem has been not only a religious and cultural center, but also an economic center and an intersection of the passage between the north and south of the West Bank, and the Gaza Strip. Before 1967, East Jerusalem extended over approximately 6.5 square kilometers. In 1967, East Jerusalem was "annexed" along with some 64.5 square kilometers of what had been the West Bank. The appropriation of Palestinian lands constitutes a cornerstone of the policy of the Judaization of Jerusalem, securing effective sovereignty over the city and its territorial, human, and cultural resources.

In 1967, more than 85 percent of the land in East Jerusalem belonged to Palestinians. Today, Israel has acquired 87 percent of the land and has vastly extended the city of Jerusalem. Palestinians are constrained to live and build if and when they obtain permission, on the remaining 13 percent of the land in East Jerusalem.

Since 1967, the demographic strategy has been to encourage Israeli Jews to live and build in East Jerusalem, while raising barriers for Palestinians who wish to do so. The Israeli policy includes expanding municipal boundaries by confiscating Palestinian owned land, while excluding the Palestinian population and using the confiscated land to build new and expand existing illegal Jewish-only settlements. Moreover, Palestinian land is often zoned as unplanned or declared a "green area," so that it cannot be used for housing.

It is very difficult for a Palestinian to get a building permit in East Jerusalem. According to the Israeli human rights organization, B'Tselem, about 88 percent of all housing units built since 1967 have been built for Israelis, in large part by public construction, while 12 percent were built for Palestinians, in large part by private construction. Because there is an enormous demand for Palestinian housing with a shortage estimated to exceed twenty thousand units, it is to be expected that illegal construction will take place. But if we build, we risk the demolition of our homes. According to veteran Israeli peace activist Amos Gvirtz, in 2007 alone, the Israeli Ministry of Interior with the Jerusalem Municipality demolished eighty-four Palestinian homes, rendering some five hundred persons homeless.[1]

The Closure of Jerusalem

Most of the more than a million foreign Christians who visit the Holy Land every year are completely unaware that since March 1993, the Israeli government has closed the city of Jerusalem to Palestinians from the West Bank and Gaza. The military closure of Jerusalem has gone hand in hand with the confiscation of Palestinian land both outside and inside Jerusalem, the building of new settlements, and what one would have to speak of as the ethnic cleansing and Judaization of the city.

The closure of East Jerusalem imposed by the Israeli authorities reinforces the isolation of the city from the remainder of the Occupied Territories and divides the West Bank into two entities. Jerusalem was always the center of Palestine, connecting the north and the south. As already noted, it is now very difficult to travel between the north and south of the West Bank because we are unable to travel freely through East Jerusalem. Also, since 1993, Palestinians of East Jerusalem cannot travel to Gaza. When there is strict closure enforcement, they cannot even enter the West Bank. Not only do Palestinians of the West Bank have no right to enter East Jerusalem, they are prevented from investing there. The closure has taken an enormous economic toll. The Palestinian merchants and businesses of East Jerusalem have increasingly had a hard time making a living, for the natural flow of business from the West Bank and Gaza has virtually stopped.

Students, medical personnel, and workers are required to request permits to go to East Jerusalem. Such permits, if given, are strictly reserved to the person, and do not include the right to use a vehicle. It is very difficult to obtain such a permit. My home in Ramallah is ten miles north of Jerusalem and I used to go to the city two or three times a week for meetings or lectures. Today, I cannot go to Jerusalem for any reason, including worship, work, education, or medical treatment.

I cannot drive my car there. If I do manage to get a permit to enter Jerusalem, I feel like a stranger in my own country. I don't recognize the new roads. I don't recognize the Hebrew names that have replaced all the traditional names.

In human terms, the policy of separation, restriction, and closure prevents the hospitals of East Jerusalem from receiving 80 percent of their patients, despite the fact that more than half of the hospitals built specifically for Palestinians are located in Jerusalem. For me and for many Palestinians, then, the closest available medical services are in Amman, Jordan. When I have needed medical treatment, I have had to travel internationally to Amman, where it is more costly and where I am away from the support of my family at the time I most need them. Even putting the issues of convenience and emotional support aside, the fact that Jerusalem health care is inaccessible puts an enormous strain on our financial resources.

The Politics of Identity Cards

The demographic control of Palestinians is related to the politics of identity cards. Over the years, using laws, regulations, court judgments, and administrative tactics, Israeli authorities have expelled thousands of persons from the city in an effort to limit the Palestinian population of Jerusalem. On one charge or another, their identity cards are revoked. Not only are these Palestinians compelled to leave their homes, but they also lose their social benefits and connection with their families. They must start life anew in another location. Between the years of 1995 and 1999, the Israeli government undertook a policy of "quiet deportation" of East Jerusalem Palestinians who moved outside the municipal bounds of Jerusalem or lived elsewhere for a number of years. The government revoked the residency permits of hundreds and hundreds of Jerusalem Palestinians and ordered them to leave their homes, without even informing them of the new law.

The politics of identity cards has become very complicated—both in Jerusalem and elsewhere in Palestine. The Israeli government policy is to limit the number of Palestinians with Jerusalem identity cards, and moreover it is confiscating the identity cards of many Palestinian Jerusalemites. If Palestinian residents of Jerusalem live elsewhere for ten years, they will lose their identity cards and be unable to return to Jerusalem. Israeli attorney Lea Tsemel saw the asymmetry of this situation and is said to have remarked in October 1996, "If Bibi Netanyahu were a Palestinian, he would never have become Prime Minister because his right of residency in Israel would have been cancelled due to his twelve-year stay in the United States." Identity cards are also used for ideological control. The implications of confiscating an identity card include losing health benefits and the right to property not only for oneself, but also for one's family.

In short, the right to residency in the city where one is born is not guaranteed for Palestinians. Many try to hang on in the face of a concerted campaign for demographic control that has been going on since 1967. Denied fair access to building permits, however, they live in extremely overcrowded conditions, paying taxes because of their Jerusalem identity cards, yet receiving few services in return.

A law passed in 2003 rules that if a Palestinian resident of East Jerusalem marries a West Bank Palestinian, he or she does not have the right to live in Jerusalem with his or her spouse unless an authorization within the frame of familial bond has been obtained from the Israeli Interior Minister. This rarely happens, so the Jerusalemite Palestinian is forced to live with his or her spouse outside the municipal boundaries of Jerusalem. So, for example, if a Palestinian woman who is a permanent resident of Jerusalem marries a West Bank Palestinian, she cannot live with her husband in Jerusalem. They both must live in the West Bank if they wish to live together. In the strictest sense, even this is not possible, since a Palestinian Israeli is not allowed to enter the West Bank without a special permit. But it happens. So, if she joins her husband to live in the West Bank, she is very likely to lose her Jerusalem residency status. Whether she lives in Jerusalem or not, it is unlikely that she will be able to obtain a Jerusalemite birth certificate for her children.

The policy of demographic control that produces such a series of harassments and requirements is clearly aimed at what can only be called the "ethnic cleansing" of Palestinians in Jerusalem.

Christian Emigration

Over the last few decades, and especially since the closure of Jerusalem, many Palestinians, especially Palestinian Christians, have decided to emigrate. The pressures of the Israeli occupation, the hard economic conditions, the ineffective and divided churches, the politics and theology of many right-wing Christian groups and Christian Zionists from abroad, and the unreliability of outside help have led to increased Christian emigration. The numbers of Palestinian Christians are already down to 42,000, a mere 3 percent of the total Palestinian population in the Occupied Territories compared with 130,000 Christians in 1967. The number of Christians in Jerusalem itself has decreased to four thousand.

The prospect of a "Holy Land Christianity" reduced to stones and ancient churches would mean that Christianity in the land of its birth is now a "museum faith" or "tourist faith," a faith without people. This is very serious and strikes a blow at the foundations of Christianity. This is also a tragedy because Palestinian life and history will be poorer without its Christian presence.

In the past few years, there have been reports of Christians being harassed and discriminated against by Muslims in Palestine. On the contrary, as a Christian Palestinian, I would say that the real story is the ways in which the policy of the Israeli government has tightened restrictions on Christian churches, especially in Jerusalem. This crisis affects many denominations and historic churches. A report in the *Christian Science Monitor* on May 4, 2004, put it this way:

> Christian churches in the Holy Land are facing an unprecedented crisis that some say is jeopardizing their future, including their capacity to maintain the faith's holy sites and charitable institutions and to educate clergy. The Israeli government has failed to renew visas or residence permits for hundreds of religious workers and has begun sending tax bills to charitable groups that have long had tax-exempt status, some since the Ottoman Empire. At the same time, the apartheid wall being built in Jerusalem and on

the West Bank is slicing through religious facilities, in some cases taking land and blocking pilgrimage routes. "All indications point to the fact that the church is slowly but surely being strangled," said an official at the Latin Patriarchate.[2]

Today, Israel prevents both Christians and Muslims from Gaza and the West Bank from worshiping in Jerusalem. Since 1967, there has been a total disruption of the pilgrimage of Christians from other Arab countries to Jerusalem. This has prevented a sense of community and exchange that has long taken place between Palestinian Christians and the twelve million Arab Christians in the Middle East. For Muslims, the disruption of pilgrimage to the Al-Aqsa and the Dome of the Rock has also been a sad reality. For all Palestinians, the increasing constriction of Jerusalem means they are deprived of educational, economic, and social interaction with Palestinians in Jerusalem. Likewise, Palestinians in Jerusalem are isolated from their brothers and sisters in the West Bank and Gaza.

Despite the fact that Jerusalem is closed to worship and pilgrimage for the Palestinians, the over one million foreign Christian visitors and pilgrims who come to the Holy Land every year mostly come and go without internalizing the gospel at all, without being involved in the passion of Christ, without responding to the needs of the sick, the hungry, and the captives even right here. Their minds seem to leap from the Holy Land of Bible times to the Jerusalem of today, with no intervening history and no sense of the history and fate of the indigenous Christian community. It is not enough that we are unknown victims, but we are also obliged to explain to our Palestinian neighbors why the most fundamentalist of these visitors issue statements of support for the State of Israel on theological grounds. Our energy is often consumed in reacting rather than acting.

Jewish visitors and pilgrims to Jerusalem are many. American Jewish groups have what they call "birthright" programs for any Jewish young person to come to the land of Israel, which is claimed as his or her birthright. These trips are often free or of very low cost, paid for by American

Jewish organizations eager to instill in young people a sense of the land that they say is theirs. But what about the birthright of my own three children and seven grandchildren and thousands of others who were born in Jerusalem and cannot even get permission to visit the city of their birth?

Palestinians today are crying for justice, and for the removal of the closure of Jerusalem to the people of the West Bank and Gaza. We are calling for a halt to all confiscation of land and water resources in Jerusalem. Yet Israel, as the powerful party, seems not to hear our cries. Israel is not abiding by international law and human rights conventions, and American presidential administrations, one after the other, do not adhere to U.S. law prohibiting economic and military aid to nations engaging in a consistent pattern of human rights violations.

American legislators who readily support Israel often do not recognize our rights as Palestinians at all. We are treated as intruders in the land of our birth. They do not recognize our right to self-determination and statehood, our right to return to our homes, our right of movement and access to places of worship in Jerusalem, and our right to adequate housing. Israel is doing all it can to dispossess us. It considers Christians and Muslims who live in occupied Palestine as resident aliens. We are not recognized as native, nor as indigenous people having the right to live where we were born.

As a Christian, I often turn to the prophets of ancient Israel, whose words are just as much a part of the Christian Bible as they are of the Tanakh, the Jewish Bible. Although spoken nearly three thousand years ago, I can hear Jeremiah speaking to them today, expressing our anguish and pain.

> I will punish this city because it is full of oppression. As a well keeps its water fresh, so Jerusalem keeps its evil fresh. I hear violence and destruction in the city. Sickness and wounds are all I see. Everyone great and small tries to make money dishonestly; even prophets and priests cheat the people. They act as if my people's wounds are only scratches. All is well, they say, when all is not well. Were they

ashamed because they did these disgusting things? No, they were not ashamed; and they do not even know how to blush. (Jer. 6:6-7, 13-15, TEV)

How often in our situation do we long to hear the voices of a contemporary Elijah pointing the prophetic finger at the Ahabs who are stealing much more than Naboth's vineyard? How often do we yearn to hear those prophets who dare say that all of us, including Palestinians and including the State of Israel, are accountable to God? The modern State of Israel is a geopolitical entity. We as Palestinian Christians cannot be silent while the State of Israel is validated theologically on biblical grounds as the sole possession of Jews. Perhaps journalists and human rights groups are doing more to break the silence—to unmask the injustice, the structural forms of violence and what is actually happening on the ground—than are the theologians, scholars, and historians. Of course, there are local and international theologians and ethicists addressing this, but they are few. While the latter continue to reflect and debate, the politicians are creating more unjust facts on the ground.

Three Faiths Toward the Future

It is no longer possible for Israel, however powerful, to solve its problems by itself, in isolation from the rest of the world, or to define its security needs unilaterally, without taking into account the security needs of its adversaries, and not least its Palestinian neighbors. Such a vision is a formula for unending conflict unless it is recognized that freedom from violence and the threat of violence is a collective necessity of the human race.

Jerusalem is a microcosm of the Israeli-Palestinian conflict. It can be either a barrier or a gateway to peace. While adherents of the three religions share an intense attachment to the city, the nature of their religious attachment is different for each religion. Moreover, religious significance rarely exists in isolation from more general cultural and political circumstances, and any discussion of relevant theological factors must be carried out in the wider context of national and international politics.

For Christians of the Holy Land, who refer to themselves as the "living stones," Jerusalem is a spiritual center and for those who live in Jerusalem it is their home. For Jews, Jerusalem and its holy places, especially the Western Wall, are seen as vital to their future. For Muslims, Jerusalem has long been a place of pilgrimage second only to Mecca and, of course, has long been home to Muslim Palestinians.

The city of Jerusalem is important to Jews, Christians, and Muslims but under the control of Israel for the last three decades. Israel has assumed absolute control over the city. It has exercised power and enacted laws in favor of Jewish interests only, and some use biblical reasons to justify our dispossession and deprivation. But no political gains should be made on religious grounds. Political problems require political solutions. We are asking to be treated according to international laws, conventions, and rights. But it often feels as if we are knocking our heads against the wall, for so many Israelis still claim they have divine rights that are over and above international legitimacy, UN resolutions, universal declarations of human rights, and the Fourth Geneva Convention. There are countless numbers of statements and resolutions by churches, church leaders, human rights organizations—both local and international—that try to share with the rest of the world this reality of what is happening to us in Jerusalem and Palestine.

The three religions speak about peace and the peace of Jerusalem, but these religions have also taken us down the road to war. And this is not just a matter of history; there is continuing fresh and bloody evidence of this fact in our world today. In defense of creed or dogma, some people would rather kill than love their brothers and sisters of different faiths and nationalities. "Thou shall not kill" loses much of its meaning in our world where violence has become not only the last resort, but increasingly the first resort when faced with problems.

Interfaith dialogue in Jerusalem among Jews, Christians, and Muslims has never been more important. But it must be a new kind of dialogue in which Christian dialogue partners are not imported from Europe and the United States. Such dialogues have been many and have reinforced the most glaring exclusion—the indigenous Palestinian Christians of the West Bank, Gaza, and Jerusalem and the Arab

Christians of the Middle East. Dialogue today should have a different agenda—not one of theology or dogma, but of common values that can help us transform our societies and ourselves. We know there can be no peace between the nations without peace between the religions.

Looking at Jerusalem today as a microcosm of the problems that we and our religious traditions have created, I believe religious people can make clear contributions to the peace of Jerusalem if we focus on common values:

- First, we must emphasize pluralism in a place where everyone has a stake in a multireligious and peaceful future.

- Second, we must all extend a hand across boundaries to those who are poor and who are victims of injustice. All people are equal before God. There are no second-class persons. And compassion is at the heart of all our religious traditions.

- Third, we must stress the importance of caring for the earth and its limited resources, even and especially here in Jerusalem. Nature is not only here to be used at the convenience of the human being; the human being is also part of nature.

- Fourth, we must try on all sides to inspire courage and hope. We will need courage to manage our fears and confront the complexity of our city. We will need hope, without which the difficulties will overwhelm us.

- Finally, we must be advocates for the rule of international law and peace, based on justice.

Jews, Christians, and Muslims should unite to preserve their presence and their rights in Jerusalem. This cannot be accomplished in a separate, chauvinistic way, but must aim to enrich the diversity of the city, and to serve with others the one God whom we all worship. We all have a role to help build a Palestinian state that coexists peacefully with its neighbors and that advocates democracy, human rights, and equality for all, including women. Our faith should compel us to work for comprehensive peace for all. Jerusalem should be a symbol of that work, a symbol of brotherhood and sisterhood, a holy place of reconciliation for humankind, and a promise of the presence of God. This is our agenda for Jerusalem. This should be our plan of action.

Although I live only ten miles from the Holy City, it requires considerable hope for me to be able to say, year after year, "Next year in Jerusalem!"

5

VIOLENCE

Do you indeed decree what is right, you gods?
Do you judge people fairly?
No, in your hearts you devise wrongs;
Your hands deal out violence on earth.
—Ps. 58:1-2

I AM ONE OF SOME NINE MILLION PALESTINIANS WORLDWIDE. Nearly sixty years ago, more than half of us were uprooted and made refugees—some of us have since been displaced multiple times. Those of us who remained in what became Israel experience discrimination in our own land. We were cast outside the course of history, our identity denied, and our very human, cultural, and historical reality suppressed. We became victims of the cruel myth: the myth that Palestine was a land without a people for a Jewish people without a land. This slogan was used to justify Jews coming from Europe to take our land.

In the search for peace in the Middle East some people begin with the Camp David agreements, others with a new status for Jerusalem. There are those who begin with the road map, while others speak of the Saudi Initiative. Others speak of the Oslo Accords or of Annapolis. Still others see peace primarily in Israel's withdrawal, in whole or in part, from lands it militarily occupied in 1967. Palestinians will always begin with the loss of our lands and our rights. This is where the search for peace must begin. For us, this is where the violence started.

Those of us who fell under Israeli occupation in 1967 in the West Bank, the Gaza Strip and East Jerusalem have since been subjected to a unique combination of military occupation, settler colonization, and systematic oppression. The infrastructure of occupation continues to entrench and expand with the building of more settlements, more bypass roads and more sections of the wall. All the while, UN Resolutions and the rulings of the International Court of Justice and International Law as they pertain to Palestine, including the Fourth Geneva Convention, continue to remain unimplemented.

The narrative of my life and of that of my Palestinian family is a narrative of exclusion. I must describe honestly the conditions of our lives. The beginning of any path to peace must be in seeing and speaking the truth: We continue to be victims of a colonialist program, that is, an exclusivist agenda, one that usurped our rights, our lands, and confiscated, as well, our historical narrative.

I have lived all my life in Ramallah, and more than half of it under Israeli military occupation. I can assure you that life has never been as difficult as it is today. "Normal life" for Palestinians living in the Occupied Territories has disappeared. The apartheid wall continues to be built on confiscated land, separating people from their lands, families, schools, hospitals, and houses of worship. Our fledgling government offices have been dynamited and bombed by F-16 fighter jets. Palestinian civilians have been forced to become human shields for Israeli soldiers. We are subjected to a policy of restrictions on our movement, a policy of intentional impoverishment, house curfews, random shootings, political assassinations, targeted killings, abductions, imprisonments, house demolitions, the illegal confiscation of our land and water resources and the destruction of our crops and thousands of our trees. More than 80 percent of our water in the West Bank is siphoned off; sometimes it is sold back to us, but at very high prices. So, you see, we are not only dealing with direct violence. We are constantly encountering structural violence that is political, economic, cultural, religious, and environmental.

Relations between Palestinians and Israelis have become hard and tense. When almost every aspect of life is framed in oppression and humiliation, moral space is diminished. Fear and insecurity overrides the building of compassion and trust. Our own humanity is threatened and role models for our children become hard to find. People are tired and depressed.

Palestinians are traumatized by the daily violence of an armed military occupation, which affects both their physical and mental health. And they see the ways in which the Israeli narrative dominates the international discourse on violence. News media outlets headline Palestinian violence and pay almost no attention to the violence Israel inflicts with impunity. Israeli violence? It is clearly not simply a response to Palestinian violence. It is a policy. It is a policy of systematic and direct violence that is intended to make life unlivable for Palestinians at all levels.

Chaim Weizmann, who was to become the first president of Israel, remarked long before the establishment of the Jewish state that the world would judge Zionists by the way they treated the Arabs of Palestine. It was a wise prediction, but more than half a century has passed and still the world has made little headway in understanding and nurturing those things that make for peace.

Why Everyone Should Be Concerned

In North America, there is still very little awareness of the depth of the violence we Palestinians have suffered in terms of the denial of our rights and self-determination. Despite the courageous advocacy of growing numbers in the international community and the justice-oriented statements of many Christian denominations, there remains much misinformation. And, quite significantly, there is the absence of effective political will on the part of the international community to resolve the Israeli-Palestinian conflict or even to view the resolution of the conflict as in the best interests of their nations. Yet, the situation is becoming more urgent with each passing day.

There are several reasons why, I believe, everyone should be concerned with this conflict and work toward peace in the Middle East.

1. It is an explosive issue. The Palestinian conflict is at the root of an explosive situation that could become a threat to world peace. It now affects the lives of millions of people in the Middle East. If it widens into regional conflict, it could affect the lives of tens of millions of people elsewhere.

2. It is an issue in which American and European governments are involved. Several governments, but especially the U.S. government, support Israel militarily, politically, and financially. Each individual has the right, if not the duty, to advocate that his or her government use its influence to promote a peace based on human rights and justice, a peace that ends the occupation, a peace that addresses the right of return and ensures security for all.

3. It is a major, long-term UN issue and one that tests the credibility and effectiveness of the United Nations. The Palestine question has been on the UN agenda since 1947. Many resolutions have been adopted, but not one implemented. Therefore, every individual has a responsibility directly or indirectly for the action or inaction of his or her own government.

4. It is one of the most serious chronic human rights issues and it tests our serious commitment to human rights. All over the world people struggle for basic human rights. The issue of basic human rights is central for the Palestinian struggle. If human rights is to mean anything anywhere, it should mean something here.

5. It is a religious issue, with implications for the integrity of people who are Jews, Christians, and Muslims alike. All three traditions stress the dignity of each human being, the justice and the judgment of God, and the importance of peacemaking. The inability of people of these faiths to make serious progress in resolving this issue stands as an indictment of us all.

When I speak to the issue of violence in Israel and Palestine, it is always with a message of hope. It is not naïve hope, but hope that grows from the witness and history of those throughout the world who refuse to submit to forces of oppression, who refuse to submit to violence, injustice, and structures of domination. Indeed, hope is revealed when truth is spoken.

Power is not a cake that is cut up and diminished the more it is shared. Power, when shared, is a relationship that enriches everyone. The great rift is not between one side and the other. Ultimately, as human beings we all belong together. Rather, the great rift is between care and carelessness, justice and injustice, mercy and mercilessness, compassion and indifference. What divides us is not difference but oppression and injustice. Difference does not destroy; rather, it is our callous ability to allow oppression and injustice to be perpetrated.

Violence and Its Deceptive Symmetry

The most basic form of deception in our context is the fabrication of a fake symmetry between occupier and occupied, between oppressor and victim, as if the claims and the power were equal on both sides. The violence of the powerful Israeli occupation army that uses live ammunition, tanks, and helicopter gunships is equated with the violence of Palestinian civilians protesting their victimization and continued loss of rights, land, and lives. Israel usually presents its military actions and policies of repression to the world as merely a justified reaction to Palestinian violence. In doing so, it frames and controls the discourse on "violence," labeling it as Palestinian. It also ensures that the very word *occupation* disappears from the dominant discourse. But the Israeli occupation is not simply a reaction to "terrorism" or a means of self-defense. It is an expression of a policy of de facto annexation that began immediately after 1967. Occupation equals violence!

Through the U.S. media and U.S. politicians one hears much about stopping the "violence." Regrettably, what is almost always meant is the violence of Palestinians, exclusively and reflexively viewed as "terror." They ignore or perhaps don't even understand the fundamental imbalance of the situation. Israel is an internationally recognized state with one of the most powerful military forces in the world, including an estimated two to three hundred nuclear warheads and an economy twenty times larger than that of the Palestinians.

This same Israel is systematically violating human rights in order to make its occupation permanent. And yet the occupation—and the massive U.S. aid that funds it—is slowly killing us all. In the two years of crisis at the start of the second intifada in 2000 and 2001, more than 646 Israelis were killed and 4,706 injured. In the same period, over 1,846 Palestinians were killed and 20,900 injured. The refusal of the international community to intervene made it complicit in the violations of human rights and war crimes.

Of course, it is also important to recognize that the victims of oppression are not blameless. Too often, they themselves become the oppressors of others. I admit that some Palestinians, in their anger and despair, have resorted to violence. I, personally, do not think that violence can lead us anywhere, neither morally nor strategically. Luckily, this has become the position not only of faith-based organizations, but many Palestinians have adopted it as well. Violence feeds upon itself. While the means of violence are not symmetrical, its results are. Violence creates a symmetry of emotion, pain, fear, mistrust. Violence creates mutual suspicion and mutual accusation.

It should surprise no one that the current Palestinian generation refuses to inherit more pain and powerlessness. Resistance is our right and our natural response to Israel's unnatural occupation. This is especially true as our young generation looks back at the so-called Oslo peace process and finds that the occupation has only become more entrenched. The illegal settler population in the West Bank, Gaza, and East Jerusalem has doubled since Oslo began in 1993 to some 400,000 persons. Some three thousand homes have been demolished, leaving over ten thousand Palestinians homeless and destitute.

We know from experience, however, that no degree of violence—whether direct or structural—can succeed in subjugating the will of a people or destroying their spirit when they are struggling for their freedom, dignity, and the right to sovereignty on their own land. All attempts at intensifying the brutality of the Israeli occupation only lead to the escalation of the conflict and increase our determination to gain our liberty.

Conflicts can only be resolved politically and legally, on the basis of parity of rights and the global rule of law. All, without double standards, should adhere to UN Security Council resolutions and international law, including the Geneva Conventions. No state is above the law. To resort to violence as an instrument of change should be rejected. However, that should by no means lead us to suppose that we should hold a passive attitude to the circumstances that confront us.

Our road to renewal and to a just peace is to be "truth-tellers." The "cover-up" is the tool of our contemporary culture. Half-truths and lies fill government halls, institutions, and the media. As Jeremiah declared, "They all deceive their neighbors, and no one speaks the truth; they have taught their tongues to speak lies" (Jer. 9:5). It is our duty to tell the truth, to uncover our scars and wounds. This requires great courage, yet it is the way by which we disarm the principalities and powers whose lies and deceit are fed by silent cooperation.

Identifying Structural Violence

As a Palestinian Quaker woman, I have confronted structures of injustice all my life. Violence, after all, is not only about war and weaponry. Political, cultural, economic, and social structures have been at work in a destructive way throughout our community. This ongoing structural violence has inflicted a great deal of suffering, both spiritual and physical.

We know on the simplest level that when an industrialized nation profits from the sale of arms to others and those arms are used for internal repression, violation of human rights, and wars within a country and between neighboring countries, that the arms economy is a party to violence. We know that the standard of living of affluent nations is often built upon the labor and exploitation of the poor. We know that the silence of people and nations contributes to a much larger war in which millions of people die every year from hunger and poverty.

In the 1970s we looked at our situation in relation to other struggles, such as the struggle in South Africa against the apartheid regime. Discerning elements of structural violence became an integral part of the analysis of violence. We began to see that structural violence is often at the heart of long-term conflict. Understanding structural violence enables us to consider our situation not merely at the level of symptoms, but more importantly at the level of underlying and systemic causes.

How do we think about the structures of violence? Is the chasm between the starving and the affluent a form of violence? Is coercion of oppression a form of violence? Is occupation a form of violence? Is the exploitation of water resources a form of violence? Is the demolition of someone's home a form of violence? Is the uprooting of ancient olive groves and countless trees a form of violence? Is the abuse of the Bible to worship the false gods of money, material wealth, race, and individualistic interests a form of violence?

Structural violence is silent. It does not show. Television captures the direct violence and most often the violence of the powerless and the hopeless, and it is headlined as terror. One basic weakness in most conceptualizations of violence in the Israeli-Palestinian conflict is the basic assumption of symmetry, which views contending parties in conflict as being equal. After all, the conflict is there because we are unequal. We are unequal in access to power, media, and influence. But we insist that we are not unequal in our rights.

How might we work to overcome the many forms of direct and structural violence? Here, I have identified several forms of violence: direct violence, economic structural violence, political structural violence, cultural structural violence, religious structural violence, and environmental structural violence. What might be the strategies for addressing these different forms of violence?

Here are a few examples that might help us think about various forms of violence and possible responses.

Forms of Violence	Possible Responses
Direct Violence Killing (e.g., targeting civilians, political assassinations) Torture Domestic violence Closure, siege Use of civilians as human shields Imprisonment without charge or trial Expulsions House demolitions	**Overcoming Direct Violence** Build multiple nonviolent strategies for resistance and confidence building (e.g., Witness for Peace, international solidarity movements, and international protection forces) Expose and delegitimize the violence of the powerful and the state Advocate ban on arms sales and production Advocate human rights and international law Economic boycott Arms embargo
Economic Structural Violence Restrictions by Israel (e.g., road blocks, closure, control of roads, house curfew) Unemployment and impoverishment Economic marginalization and exclusion Exploitation of water, land, people's work Destruction of civil society and infrastructure No protection	**Overcoming Economic Structural Violence** Advocate economic rights, water rights, land rights, and ecological sustainability Create jobs Advocate fair trade Advocate right sharing of resources
Political Structural Violence Military occupation Settlements Denial of self-determination, sovereignty, right of return Closures Siege Encagement Fragmentation	**Overcoming Political Structural Violence** Advocate political rights according to international law and UN resolutions Advocate human, water, and land rights Advocate for self-determination

Cultural Structural Violence	Overcoming Cultural Structural Violence
Stereotyping of Palestinians, Arabs, women in the media, education, language Anti-Arabism Discrimination of women Imposition of other cultures and their value systems (e.g., patriarchal culture, Western culture) Authoritarianism and glorification of militarism/the violence of the state and direct violence Destruction/shelling of cultural heritage sites, both archeological and architectural	Media and education strategies building on authentic witness Dialogue Encounter Participation in decision making Learn about Palestinian history and heritage
Religious Structural Violence	Overcoming Religious Structural Violence
Language (chosenness) Disunity among the churches Christian Zionism Fundamentalisms Demonization of Islam Negation of Arab and Middle Eastern Christians (e.g., pilgrimages without contact with local Christians, missionary movements)	Expose the political chauvinism of fundamentalist movements and their stand against women, as well as their religious and political exclusivity Contextual and liberation theology based on nonviolence Work for ecumenism and unity Disassociate ourselves from fundamentalisms Education on Islam (e.g., among Christians) Alternative pilgrimages
Environmental Structural Violence	Overcoming Environmental Structural Violence
Confiscation and destruction of agricultural land Uprooting of trees Pirating and diversion of water resources Restrictions on water well drilling and water capture Dumping of solid and toxic waste in Occupied Territories Settlement sewage onto village lands Restrictions on movement and settler violence prevent farmers access to their lands Damaged infrastructure leads to public health problems such as no clean water and no refrigeration for vaccines	Adherence to international environmental conventions and protocols (e.g., Convention on Combating Desertification, Convention of Conservation of Biodiversity, Kyoto Protocol) Adherence to Geneva Conventions which call for protection of natural resources of Occupied Territories Observe international human rights standards which call for clean water and sanitation Support international environmental organizations working in the Occupied Territories Eco-friendly tourism Support greening campaigns in Occupied Territories Recycle, reuse, reduce

The goal of those who use violence, whether it be freelance violence or state-supported violence, is to fill our mental and emotional space with rage, fear, powerlessness, and despair, and to cut us off from the sources of life and hope. I have chosen to take an active part in the struggle to resist all forms of violence, and to do so nonviolently. Even though many of our own responses call for advocacy, support, and education, I am convinced that this transformation of consciousness is the prerequisite for real change.

I have learned over the years that the struggle to subvert violence and strengthen human rights is global. What we are able to do in one place is done on behalf of people everywhere. At the same time, our global responsibilities and relationships have a local face, and no matter where we live we can work for human rights and a culture of nonviolence. The kinships we form serve as the prototype of a new community that knows no national, racial, or gender boundaries.

We must not give up, for to give up is to give in to the forces of violence. Our situation in Palestine calls upon all our resources—physical, mental, and spiritual. And in the darkest nights of the soul, we Palestinians seek the affirmation and action of people everywhere. This is especially true now as governments and power systems have failed us. Due to power politics, the absence of will, and shortsighted self-interest, they have failed to provide the protection that is our right and their responsibility. We must continue to fan the embers of light no matter how small they are, because these embers of light give hope to those in the forefront of the struggle and will keep the work for justice and peace in the Middle East alive.

6

NONVIOLENCE

I CALL MYSELF A QUAKER OR A FRIEND. And Friends, throughout history, have maintained a testimony to nonviolence. War, we say, is contrary to the teachings of Christ. Therefore, we are challenged to live in the presence of that power which wins through love rather than through war. This is no easy testimony. It has three aspects:

1. To refuse to take part in acts of war ourselves.
2. To strive to remove the causes of war.
3. To use the way of love open to us to promote peace and to heal wounds.

As Quakers we believe that there is something of God in every person. Why, then, is it so hard for us to see what is of God in one another? Both sides in any conflict often have difficulty seeing the other at all, let alone seeing that of God in the other. But we must realize that those who benefit from the structures of oppression are dependent on the people they oppress and are equally in need of liberation and God's grace. It seems to me that too often the will and strength to end the oppression and violence comes from those who bear the oppression and violence in their own lives and very rarely from privileged and powerful persons and nations.

Living under military occupation has forced me to go through deep self-searching. I have been confronted with three loyalties. The first loyalty is to Christ, who calls us to love our enemy. The second loyalty is to our fellow human beings whenever they are in need or trouble. The third loyalty is to our country, its people, and its way of life. This prevents us from being willing to aid our invader. In our situation, no one can set rules for us to follow, but what we can do is testify that, in our experience, the spirit of God leads us into truth and gives us the guidance and courage we need in every situation.

Our analysis of nonviolent resistance must begin, of course, by taking a look into ourselves. Gandhi often spoke of "turning the search-light inward," meaning that the outward situation often reflects our inward state of conflict. We need to see this clearly. It requires great self-denial and the surrendering of our selves to God to be committed to peace and to nonviolent action to bring about change. This technique may have no immediate positive effect, and it may lead to outward defeat. Whether successful or not, it will bring suffering. But if we believe in nonviolence as the true way of peace and love, we must make it a principle not only of individual but also of national and universal conduct.

Nonviolence should not, however, instill feelings of moral superiority, because we know how soon we may stumble when we are put to the test. We may talk about peace, but if we are not transformed inwardly, if we still are motivated by greed, if we are nationalistic, if we are bound by beliefs and dogmas for which we are willing to destroy others, we cannot have peace in the world.

I believe that we are called to conversion: to be converted to the struggle of women and men everywhere who have no way to escape the unending fatigue of their labor and the daily denial of their human rights and human worth. We must be converted, so to speak, to a new vision of human dignity, what we call "that of God" in each person, even in those we oppose. We must let our hearts be moved by the anguish and suffering of the other.

Early on in my struggles with living nonviolently in a situation of violence, I found myself at a crossroads. I needed to know in my own deepest convictions whether I really did believe in the power of nonviolence to transform a situation of conflict. My own questions and experiences seemed to pull me in different directions and the whole journey seemed simply too difficult. My life seemed to have turned into a jigsaw puzzle for which I could not find all the pieces. I had been taught to love my enemy but, sometimes, those words simply increased the tension within myself. How can I have peace within when I worry so much about life in general and the lives of my family members? How can I have peace within when others call my people terrorists and justify our oppression by quoting the Bible? How can I have peace within when our movement is restricted in our own country, when walls are built to imprison us and separate us from one another?

My questions are like those of many of my fellow Palestinians. We have been working for a long time to end oppression and occupation and have, thus far, not secured our rights. It is discouraging. Fear and loss surround us, and many forces are at work to make us feel marginalized and disempowered. At best the work ahead seems overwhelming.

In the midst of privation, anxiety, and suffering, I found that my hope was simply to acknowledge my dependence upon God. I thought often of the affirmation of Paul in his letter to the Philippians: "I have learned to be content with whatever I have. I know what it is to have little, and I know what it is to have plenty. In any and all circumstances I have learned the secret of being well-fed and of going hungry, of having plenty and of being in need. I can do all things through him who strengthens me" (Phil. 4:11b-13). I know, wherever I am, whether in affluent circumstances or in poverty, whether I have personal liberty or not, that I am under the guiding hand of God and that God has a service for me to render.

As Palestinian women, we have a special burden and service. We are constantly being told to be peaceful. But the inner peace of which I speak is not simply being nice, or being passive, or permitting oneself to be trampled upon without protest. It is not passive nonviolence, but the nonviolence of courageous action.

Practical Nonviolence

For me, nonviolence is a religious conviction and a way of life. But I believe it is also highly practical. There is no other effective way to change the dynamics of attack and counterattack, even for someone who does not hold this conviction. Look at it: violence has produced counterviolence. Violence has become a cycle of despair for both sides. And, practically speaking, violence is not strategically useful, because we and our opponents have asymmetrical access to power. In the West Bank and the Gaza Strip we do not have an army. Israel is a nuclear power and one of the four largest producers of arms in the world. What is the alternative? To submit? To become bitter? To collaborate? To do nothing about the forces that control our lives? Rather than resorting to desperate forms of violence, I am convinced that active nonviolence is still the only path to resist the occupation and the structures of domination.

How can I interpret this nonviolence to my children and to my students when we have all been the victims of violence? This is the challenge. How do we deal with the violence that is implicit in the structures that surround us? How do I interpret nonviolence to the skeptics among Palestinians when they see that the violence of Israel has brought about changes that benefit those who employ it, while nonviolence appears to permit others to take over our homeland? How do I show them that our faith, our pacifism, can be a practical faith, an effective pacifism?

Year after year, facing the challenges of land and water, political freedom and the freedom even to move from place to place, some of my people have opted to withdraw. They either withdraw internally from the conflict or they physically leave Palestine and withdraw externally. Many have responded in this manner because they truly perceive their situation as intolerable and hopeless. Regardless of the motivation, withdrawal cushions us from feeling the full impact of our situation. But it also cuts us off from the information and the observations vital to our survival as a people. When we withdraw, our gifts and our perceptions get buried. The realities of domination go unchallenged, leading neither to inner nor outer transformation.

Some people, of course, have chosen to accommodate, comply, or manipulate. When we manipulate, we have the illusion of being in control. We can reap some rewards, but in doing so we are accepting the system's terms, its unspoken rules and values, including the often negative values it accords to us. Manipulation does not challenge the low value the system places on us as individuals and as a people. In order to manipulate the system of Israeli power, we cannot be ourselves, express our true feelings, or share our real perceptions; we literally mask ourselves. Manipulation may get us some of the system's rewards, but it neither liberates us individually nor transforms the structures of domination.

The alternative is to resist. Resistance challenges the system's values and categories. Resistance speaks its own truth to power, and shifts the ground of struggle to its own terrain. Resistance is often thought of as negative. However, resistance is the refusal to be neglected and disregarded. Today, Palestinians find themselves embedded in structures that neglect and discard their humanity and human rights, and only acts of resistance can transform these structures. And I, along with many others, have opted for the path of active nonviolent resistance. To resist is to be human, and yet nonviolent resistance is not easy. It requires constant, hard work. Indeed, it is not easy to sustain the path of nonviolent resistance for years and years, over many issues. None of us can resist all the time, in every area of life. We must choose our battles, meaning we must choose the priorities of struggle.

Nonviolent Resistance

Whenever I am in the United States, I realize that many Americans are aware of the efforts of Israeli peace groups; however, they seem to be largely unaware of Palestinian peacemaking efforts. They ask, "Where is the Palestinian peace movement?" Others get caught up in the larger, global culture of anti-Arabism and assume that Arabs are violent by nature. Certainly, there is very little fair reporting and critical discussion in the mainstream media, academia, and religious circles on this topic. Most have probably heard very little about the long-standing and rapidly growing nonviolent resistance movement in Palestine.

The word *sumoud* in Arabic might be best translated as "steadfastness." It plays an incredibly important part in Palestinian culture and self-identity. This is especially true given present-day, as well as historical, challenges to the self-determination of the Palestinian people. To practice *sumoud* means to remain steadfast on one's land and, more generally, to remain steadfast in service to one's homeland and to the struggle for freedom. For example, given the current grave circumstances, just waking up every morning with the determination to carry on with one's daily routine and to hold fast to one's humanity in spite of the challenges and dangers in movement—walking through military checkpoints to get to work, driving your children past army tanks to get to school, taking your herd out to graze despite physical and verbal abuse of Israeli settlers—is to practice *sumoud* or to be *samid* or *samida*.

On an almost daily basis, in villages and cities in the West Bank, there are nonviolent demonstrations taking place to resist the wall whose path is confiscating lands, splitting villages, and destroying economic and social structures. Hundreds of men and women, old and young, have bravely sat in front of bulldozers and placed themselves between the machinery and the construction site. Many of them believe they have nothing to lose, for if the wall succeeds along the current path, they will be without access to the land passed down to them by their ancestors. The villagers of Yanun and Qawawis were forcibly expelled from their villages by settlers but have returned to live in their homes despite settler harassment. Many villagers have faced hundreds of canisters of tear gas as they stand to protest the uprooting of more than one thousand olive trees to make way for the wall. All of them are demonstrating what we Palestinians call *sumoud,* their determination to live on their land and be treated as human beings with equal rights.

When I was an officer in the world YWCA, I often visited three Palestinian refugee camps because the YWCA has many projects there. On one occasion I was visiting Jalazone refugee camp in the Ramallah district during the first intifada after three long weeks of curfew and closure. The camp residents had been collectively punished by having their electricity cut off and their supply of gas curtailed. Women told me how determined they were to find a way to bake their own bread. They collected wood and rubbish and made a communal fire, which was kept alight by burning old shoes and rags. When the Israeli soldiers came to put the fire out and throw away the dough, the women resisted, shouting, "Go tell your leaders that no matter what you do, no matter what kind of restrictions you impose on us, we will not allow our children to starve. We will find a way to bake bread, and all your efforts to destroy our spirits are not going to succeed. What God has created, no one can destroy!" What a testimony! This is *sumoud*.

Nonviolent resistance has also meant noncompliance with the military occupation. At the individual level, this has translated into my long-standing commitment to use locally grown and locally produced products. It means boycotting Israeli goods whenever possible, most especially those products produced in illegal Israeli colonies or settlements. Similarly, I have always been an advocate of morally responsible investment or selective divestment. I cannot participate even indirectly in supporting and enabling unjust policies and the violation of basic human rights. Boycotts, divestment, and sanctions are nonviolent means for individuals, churches, academic institutions, cities, and corporations to make a difference and to highlight the need for adherence to international law and the rapid achievement of a just peace. Divestment means we ourselves will not be party to businesses that profit from occupation.

Nonviolence in the Palestinian struggle is certainly not new. However, there is a growing movement not only of nonviolent resistance, but also of nonviolent direct action. In 2005, a national conference developing a Palestinian nonviolent strategy was held in Ramallah, bringing together hundreds of community leaders engaged in nonviolent activities. Entire villages are asking to be trained in nonviolent methods. This trend builds upon tactics used in the first intifada, such as tax resistance, boycotts, sit-ins, and strikes. The world is often unaware of these movements, for they do not create the kind of news that the media sees.

Nonviolence is threatening to the powers that be because nonviolence undermines their pretense to moral authority. Nonviolence reconceptualizes power and it gives the ordinary person power to effect change. Nonviolence exposes and then challenges the structures of domination and not just the overt symptoms. It then, in turn, requires the oppressor to examine how they, too, are victims of the very violence that they impart. For in the end, the violence of occupation is killing—morally, physically, and spiritually—both peoples.

The Choice of Nonviolence

I have dedicated most of my life, for nearly forty years, to sharing the truth. That means offering the narrative of our lives, a narrative that so often is forgotten or neglected. That also means networking by forming alliances between like-minded people and organizations involved in the various struggles around the globe. Ultimately, I have learned that the nonviolent struggle for justice is one struggle, and that an action to subvert violence and strengthen human rights in one place is an action on behalf of people everywhere.

I have managed to find peace within—without having to embrace with approval the violence around me. Love of one's enemies forces me to recognize that my enemy, too, is a child of God. This realization is necessary if our enemies are ever to make the changes we are requiring of them. It is really only in the light of love that I am liberated to work for peace and freedom.

Without question, this continues to be one of the hardest paths that I must walk on my spiritual journey. Thankfully, there have been milestones along the way, moments of pure joy when my soul has been washed with peace, when I have been filled with strength, when my pacifist approach to life has worked. I know that even in the midst of persecution we can find ourselves possessed by the power of divine forgiveness. There is always a subtle pride in clinging to our hatreds, reminding ourselves that they are justified, imagining that no one else in human history has suffered as we. God's forgiving love can burst like a flare—even in the midst of our grief and hatred—and free us to love.

What is that inner force that drives us, that provides regeneration and perseverance to speak the truth, that desperately needs to be spoken in this moment of history? Today I am older, my health poor, my body fragile, and yet, as do so many others, I believe that I have no choice but to bear witness to what is happening in my land, to expose the structures of violence and domination, to bring them out into the light, and thereby undercut their power. What is that inner force driving us, providing regeneration and perseverance to speak the truth that so desperately needs to be spoken in this moment in history? If I deserve credit for courage, it is not for anything I do here, but for continuing in my daily struggle under occupation on so many fronts, for remaining *samideh* (steadfast) and, all the while, remaining open to love, to the beauty of the earth, and contributing to its healing when it is violated.

We spend our daily lives as persons and as communities in the midst of violence. We find ourselves, willingly or unwillingly, participating in social organizations that practice violence and embody its principles. For those who opt for violence against injustice, can we say that we would rather see them die than defend themselves? Who will throw the first stone of condemnation? Who is morally superior? When we condemn those who opt for violence, are we demonizing others in order that we may relish our own sense of greater worthiness? Are we thus relieving ourselves of our responsibility for the sin of dealing with our brothers and sisters as if they were less than human?

As we opt for violence or nonviolence in our revolution, we understand that the liberty to choose is not always available. Pacifists and nonpacifists committed to the struggle for a just future should, I believe, regard each other as allies on most issues. The divisions that separate these two groups do not approach in magnitude those that exist between those on the side of liberation and those who support the oppressive structures of the status quo. As Christians, the gospel compels us to withhold support from oppressive structures and, in any case, such support is an impossible alternative for us today.

There are, of course, many contemporary ideas on revolution. But these revolutions have involved surface change: the transfer of power from one personality to another; the replacement of one tyranny by another. A real revolution must concern itself with the triumph of human values and of human rights. Christian teachings are relevant to such a revolution. Although these teachings are essentially nonviolent, they can never be characterized as encouraging passivity or disengagement in the face of injustice. Rather, Christ's teachings are activist, highly political, and often controversial. They sometimes involve dangerous forms of engagement in social and political conflict.

In this struggle, it is my belief that means and ends should be consistent. I cannot endorse acts of violence in my day-to-day confrontations and, at the same time, be taken seriously when I speak of an ideal for the future that exalts wisdom, sensitivity, fairness, and compassion as basic requirements for running the world. The peculiar strength of nonviolence comes from the dual nature of its approach: the offering of respect and concern on the one hand while meeting injustice with noncooperation and defiance on the other. These seemingly contradictory impulses—to rage against while simultaneously refusing to destroy—combine to create a force worthy of nothing less than a revolution. By this I mean not just a reshuffling of death-dealing powers, but a genuine restructuring of the society in which we live.

Sulha, Reconciliation

Finger pointing and blame is the fuel of the cycle of conflict. But the prophet Isaiah gives hope to those who would find another way.

> If you remove the yoke from among you, the pointing of the finger, the speaking of evil, if you offer your food to the hungry and satisfy the needs of the afflicted, then your light shall rise in the darkness and your gloom be like the noonday. The Lord will guide you continually, and satisfy your needs in parched places, and make your bones strong; and you shall be like a watered garden, like a spring of water, whose waters never fail. Your ancient ruins shall be rebuilt; you shall raise up the foundations of many generations; you shall be called the repairer of the breach, the restorer of streets to live in. (Isa. 58:9-12).

How do we take away the yoke and the pointing of the finger? What are the demands of reconciliation? I cannot reconcile myself to structures of domination and oppression, covered over with words of peace and reconciliation. To me, it is hypocrisy when words of peace and healing are preached without regard to any genuine change in the oppressive situation created by the powerful over the weak. Too often in our talk about peace and reconciliation, the victimized are called to forgive and reconcile in a way that perpetuates rather than rectifies the root causes of injustice, alienation, and division. Reconciliation can mean a collapse into acceptance of the status quo because of the belief that nothing can be done.

Real reconciliation involves a fundamental repair to human lives, especially to those who have suffered. It requires restoring the dignity of the victims of violence. Reconciliation contains four dimensions: political, economic, psycho-social, and spiritual. Christ did not merely announce the good news that the sick can be healed. He healed and in that act proclaimed the Kingdom. Word and deed are one. They are inseparable. Reconciliation is central to the gospel and those of us who are Christians must be active in reconciling—in repairing lives and proclaiming the good news. Reconciliation as a way of transformation challenges us to resist the temptation simply to rearrange the furniture, whether that rearrangement is in the structures of our psyche or those of our planet.

But the fact remains that many Israelis do not feel guilt for what they did; they do not feel that they have done anything wrong because of their Zionist ideology. Therefore, reconciliation is not an issue for them. Many talk to us about reconciliation by suggesting a hasty peace. They speak of reconciliation instead of liberation or reconciliation as a managed process. These calls want us, the victims of violence, to let bygones be bygones and exercise a Christian forgiveness. In trivializing and ignoring the history of suffering, the victims are forgotten and the causes of suffering are never uncovered and confronted. Reconciliation is not a hasty peace that tries to escape the examination of the causes of suffering. If the causes are not addressed, suffering is likely to continue. The wheel of violence keeps turning and more and more people get crushed.

Let me share with you our Palestinian and Arab way of making peace and granting forgiveness. If my neighbor or any member of the community has violated my dignity in any way or even has taken my land or injured any of my family members, the first step in this nonviolent form of peacemaking is for the person who wronged me to choose a mediator, someone who is well respected in the society for his or her values of justice and reconciliation. Then we proceed in the following way:

1. A date is set to visit me in my home in the presence of my extended family members. Reconciliation involves community participation.

2. The person who wronged me will come with the mediator and his/her extended family members. Reconciliation involves this expression of humility.

3. The person who has wronged me recognizes the hurt that was done. Then a commitment is made to repair the damage and forgiveness is asked for. Reconciliation involves the heartfelt expression of truth and a commitment to repair.

4. The mediator takes the responsibility of executing the repairing of the damage. There is a trusted third party to see to it that reparations are followed through.

5. Then forgiveness is given ("*ahli samah imnah*") by saying, "You are in our home. You are one of us and we take it upon ourselves to help and protect the person who has done us wrong." It is then proclaimed: "Forgiveness is a gift from God" ("*samah min Allah*"). Forgiveness is essential for real reconciliation.

6. Finally, all share in eating together, breaking bread together, which is a commitment of friendship and sharing rather than enmity and exploitation.

This way of making peace and reconciliation, called *sulha*, respects and restores the dignity of both parties. Rather than continue a cycle of humiliation and violence, *Sulha* takes steps toward a new relationship of equity and respect. In my humble experience, I have found that peculiar strength of nonviolence comes from the dual nature of its approach:

offering respect and concern on the one hand while meeting injustice with noncooperation and defiance on the other.

Let us nurture the growth of a breakthrough community of friends that crosses boundaries, deconstructs the dominant ideology that normalizes sin and injustice, and shapes an alternative praxis of mutuality.

> We form a circle of hope
> We pass the flame to one another
> If my candle goes out, yours will light it.
> Together we make a brighter light.
> And each candle promises something of its own:
> That darkness is not the last word.
> —David McCauley

7

WAR, PEACE, AND JUSTICE

LAMENTATIONS AND AFFIRMATIONS

What does the Lord require of you but to do justice, and to love kindness, and to walk humbly with your God?—Mic. 6:8

WHEN I GREET YOU IN ARABIC I start with *salaam*, "Peace"—when I say goodbye, it is "Go in God's peace." So the word *peace* is central in our language. As a people and as persons we yearn for peace. We greet one another with peace. We pray for peace. We are called to be peacemakers.

Peace, compassion, faithfulness, and self-control are qualities strengthened in the holy month of Ramadan. "Peace be to you" is the common greeting. "Peace to our world" and "Working together for peace" have been mottoes of many organizations. Some years ago, the United Nations designated an International Year of Peace. Christians all over the world celebrate the birth of Jesus in our land with the song of the angels, "Peace on earth."

But what is peace? Is it the cessation of conflict? Not in the real world. Conflict is an inevitable fact of daily life—internal, interpersonal, intergroup, and international conflict. Peace consists in consistently being able to deal creatively with inevitable conflict. Peace is the process of working to resolve conflicts in such a way that both sides win, with increased harmony as the outcome of the conflict and its resolution. Peace is based on respect, cooperation, and well-being. Peace is the presence of social justice.

The most crucial issue of the Israeli-Palestinian conflict is that of justice. Justice, like peace, means different things to different people. Some define justice very narrowly. For them it means the establishment of rights based on laws or rules. Others take a broader view of justice, righteousness and equality, wholeness and well-being. Under the narrow understanding of justice, the wealthy and powerful are able to make the laws and then have the laws interpreted in their favor. In a strict sense, they say they are obeying the law, but they are taking advantage of the poor and powerless. In occupied Palestine, laws are made and manipulated by the powerful to make life difficult and unlivable for Palestinians living in Israel and in the occupied territories.

Coming from a land where the words of our great prophets ring through the hills, I can see that the issues of injustice are not really new. Only the people and situations are new. "Listen, you rulers of Israel!" says the prophet Micah, "Should you not know justice? You who hate the good and love the evil" (Mic. 3:1). "Woe to you who join house to house, who add field to field until there is room for no one but you," cries the prophet Isaiah (5:8) "Ah, you who make iniquitous decrees, who write oppressive statutes, to turn aside the needy from justice and to rob the poor of my people of their right, that widows may be your spoil and that you may make the orphans your prey!" (Isa. 10:1-2).

The very words *peace* and *justice* go together, so clearly have we seen the relationship between them. Peace is not only the absence of war, but it is the absence of dire poverty and hunger. Peace is freedom from sickness and disease. It is employment and health. Peace is based on a deep sense of human equality and basic justice. Peace is when we have no fear to assemble, to worship, to work, to speak and publish the truth, even to the powerful. Peace is hope for our future and the future of all God's children and all God's world. Peace is *salaam*, well-being for all, equality and respect for human rights. Peace is when everybody feels at home and is accepted, without barriers based on age, class, sex, race, religion, or nationality. Peace is that fragile harmony that carries with it the experience of struggle, the endurance of suffering, and the strength of love.

There is so much that is gathered into the word *peace*. Peace is costly and must not be misunderstood to mean a patchwork solution to the conflicts of the world. Peace is not submission, nor is it silent acceptance of what goes on around us. Peace is not only the peace of governments, their plans and initiatives, which we have been hearing about for so long.

The Process of Peace

I have watched anxiously the unfolding of the Middle East Peace Process (MEPP). The Palestinian people have accepted an extraordinary set of compromises in most of these, compromises required of no other participant. At the outset, we were not represented by the PLO, no one from East Jerusalem was allowed to attend, no one from outside the West Bank and Gaza was allowed to participate even though Palestinians are one people, half of whose number live in forced exile outside Palestine. At that time, Israel was not committing itself to withdrawal, to end the military occupation, to dismantle settlements, or to Palestinian self-determination, and the right of return. Such a vision is, of course, a formula for unending conflict. Cosmetic peace was then and still is not enough.

The Oslo Accords were hailed as a great step in the Peace Process. The ceremony held on September 13, 1993, on the White House lawn in Washington, D.C., had all the outer signs of an agreement signed by two equal partners. The famous handshake between Yitzhak Rabin and Yasser Arafat was seen around the world.

However, this equality is not reflected in the actual documents signed at the ceremony. The most obvious inequality in the Oslo-Washington agreements concerned the PLO's pledge to recognize Israel and to stop all violent acts against it without Israel's pledge to stop its soldiers from killing Palestinians, or to drop any of its oppressive measures in the Occupied Territories, or to commit itself to end occupation, or to protect Palestinian human rights.

The Oslo Accords presented the world with misleading images of peace and we were left with a difficult and hard reality on the ground. The international media referred to the Accords as historic because they brought peace and reconciliation. I often quote the words of the prophet Ezekiel who speaks of false prophets, "Because they mislead my people, saying, 'Peace,' when there is no peace" (13:10) or the words of Isaiah 59:14-15, "Justice is turned back, and righteousness stands at a distance; for truth stumbles in the public square, and uprightness cannot enter. Truth is lacking, and whoever turns from evil is despoiled." To have peace we must tell the truth; without truth-telling there is no peacemaking.

It is not easy for me to analyze the Peace Process and its shortcomings, because the local and international media have made it seem as if whoever is against the Process is against peace, irrational, and immoderate. One might even be labeled a fanatic or terrorist. When I spoke about the Oslo Accords in September of 1993 in Selly Oak Colleges in Birmingham, England, and 1994 in Sweden, many people could not understand why a Quaker and a peace activist would warn of a sad outcome rather than rejoice. Why? I had to explain over and over again that Palestinian and Arab views are rarely included in the mainstream media. For that reason, there was what seemed to be unanimity in the public discourse of the West that the Peace Process envisioned by Oslo was a good thing.

The years since Oslo have given Palestinians responsibility for the people and civil services of Palestine, while maintaining Israeli control over the land, water, and natural resources, the borders, and all passage of people and goods. Israel controls the economy, maintaining hundreds of checkpoints and instituting a system that sometimes requires that goods be loaded and unloaded as many as seven times between Hebron and Nablus, even though both are located in the occupied West Bank. While Israeli settlers were withdrawn from Gaza, Israel has complete control over what goes in and out of Gaza. Trucks loaded with farm goods for markets in Europe or the West Bank can be held at the border of Gaza for so long that all the produce rots in the truck. Gaza is the most densely populated place on earth and is, in practical terms, under the complete control of the Israeli military. According to human rights organizations, Gaza is still under occupation, even though the settlers have left. The occupation has not ended. That point was unfortunately illustrated by the Israeli military invasion during the summer of 2006.

Under the Oslo Accords, Israel was to create a "safe passage" between the West Bank and Gaza, so that Palestinians could move more freely. Israel never implemented this safe passage route, thereby isolating the Gaza Strip from the rest of Palestinian territory. Palestinians require Israeli military permits to travel within the West Bank, or between the West Bank and Gaza, or into Israel. Palestinians in Gaza also require Israeli permission to cross international boundaries to visit other countries. These permits are very difficult to obtain. Permission to travel out of the Tel Aviv airport is only granted for exceptional cases. For all intents and purposes, Palestinians from the West Bank can only exit via Amman and via Rafah to Egypt.

Looking back, one analyst wrote, "Oslo can only be genuinely understood as an economic, political and disciplinarian restructuring of Israel's relationship with the occupied territories, based on the unanimity of given Zionist agendas within Israel."[1] Or, according to Edward Said, "How do you spell apartheid? O-S-L-O."[2]

When the military attorney warned him about this, former Israeli prime minister Ehud Barak is said to have answered, "No international law can change our approach. Our decisions are not made according to international precedents but according to our needs and interests." Neither is Israeli law Barak's frame of reference when it comes to deciding the legitimacy of any settlement, despite the fact that the "rule of law" was a central issue in his 1999 election campaign. Only seven "strongholds" out of the forty-two built after the Wye River Agreement in 1998 were declared illegal by Israel—that is, as not having permission from the Israeli government to exist. And only two of the seven illegal settlements were evacuated.

Illegal under international law, settlements are one of the most dangerous components of the apartheid system. Settlement growth is driven by political and ideological considerations that serve the strategic, military, and economic interests of Israel as well as its scheme of national assertiveness. As already noted, the number of settlers has reached a total of more than 400,000, of which more than 180,000 live in Jerusalem. Before 2004, more than six thousand lived in eighteen settlements in Gaza. These settlements are united by a system of highways or bypass roads and industrial areas that prevent continuity between Palestinian towns and villages and have also been built upon confiscated Palestinian land. There are 177 settlements in the West Bank, including Jerusalem.

Israel has permitted these settlements to cause environmental degradation to adjacent Palestinian communities. Untreated sewage, for example, is often allowed to run into the valleys below settlements, threatening the agriculture and health of neighboring Palestinian towns and villages. The very existence of these settlements is a direct violation of internationally binding agreements and regulations, as international humanitarian law explicitly prohibits the occupying power to make permanent changes that do not benefit the occupied population.

Not only does our land continue to be confiscated, but also our water resources. Israel controls all the water resources of the West Bank and the Gaza Strip, siphoning at least 85 percent for its own use, selling our water back to us and leaving us with only 15 percent of our own water for all our needs, domestic and agricultural. Israel's control of the two main water aquifers has enabled Israelis to enjoy "a massively disproportionate supply of water," more than four times as much water as do Palestinians. As a result, Palestinians have become less and less able to use water for crop irrigation or even to water backyard family vegetable plots, let alone flower gardens, and trees. All the while, Jewish settlers water their grass lawns and fill their swimming pools with our water. In Hebron, for example, 70 percent of the water goes to 8,500 settlers, and only 30 percent is allocated to the city's 250,000 inhabitants.[3]

As we have seen, Israel continues to confiscate and build on Arab land in East Jerusalem as part of the "Judaization" of the city. Arab Jerusalemites are not only deprived of their land but are also often denied building permits. Many suffer from house demolitions and the loss of their Jerusalem residency rights and accompanying social services. Since March 1993, Israel has closed off the city of East Jerusalem from the rest of the West Bank. Palestinians who are not officially residents of the city are not allowed to enter Jerusalem without a proper permit issue from the Israeli military authorities. This closure essentially divides the West Bank into north and south cantons and has greatly increased the fragmentation of the Palestinian community.

I am a pacifist. I declared publicly, as early as 1975, at the Nairobi Fifth Assembly of the World Council of Churches that my aspirations for peace and reconciliation are based on the mutual recognition of the rights of both Palestinians and Israelis, including a two-state solution according to International Law and UN resolutions, the right of return for Palestinian refugees, and equality for Palestinians living in Israel.

Mine was a lonely voice then, and I was asked by many church leaders not to stick my neck out on this issue. However, I did not stop. I continue until this day because the cries of my people for peace with justice are loud and clear, and my will to resist injustice has not been defeated. I do admit that often I feel tired, frustrated, and drained, but my relationships with supporters in the peace and justice movement all over the world give me the strength to go on. In Israel-Palestine the relationship of peace and justice could not be clearer.

Can we have peace without self-determination and sovereignty? Can we have peace without our land and water? Can we have peace while Israel imposes restrictions that choke our economic life? Can we have peace with endless roadblocks, closures, isolation, and unemployment? Can we have peace with no protection whatsoever from the arbitrary use of force?

Can we have peace when millions of Palestinian refugees still live in refugee camps in the Gaza Strip and the West Bank, in Jordan, Syria, and Lebanon? The refugees had hoped that the Oslo Accords would address the issue of their right of return and compensation, which is a basic human right. Refugees suffer from overcrowding, poverty, scarcity of water, lack of a sanitation system, and unemployment, as well as a decrease in the services offered by UNWRA, the United Nations Works and Relief Agency for Palestinian Refugees. The situation of refugees in Lebanon and the Gaza Strip is worse than those in refugee camps in Jordan and the West Bank, but all share the frustration of growing unemployment and the lack of progress on the refugee question in the political negotiations. The Palestinian refugees would like to participate in setting the agenda in defense of their rights according to UN Resolution 194 and international law that supports their right to property and compensation.

The Universal Declaration of Human Rights does not allow for racial, ethnic, or religious segregation. That is racism. Europeans are alarmed if right-wing political or religious leaders encourage racism and exclusiveness. But what we Palestinians cannot understand is how in our own country, in our own land, we can be denied water or land or building permits or the right to free movement or right of return or self-determination all because we are not Jewish. And how can this be tolerated by the enlightened world in light of the many UN resolutions that have been passed condemning these practices and demanding justice for Palestinians?

Why are Palestinians living in the Occupied Territories forced to live in bantustans without the right to resist because resistance is interpreted as terrorism? And why is this not called apartheid? Is this racism or is it a peace process? Why should we have to drop our priorities for independence, statehood, or human rights just to improve Israeli security? Is this really democracy? Is this equality? Is this a mutuality that will discourage all forms of direct and structural violence and bring about peace and reconciliation?

Can we go on endorsing a peace process that assumes an asymmetry between us and does not treat our peoples as equal? After all, the conflict is there because of the incompatibility between the two parties. Can we go on with these arrangements while Israel dictates rather than negotiates and does so without regard for the deteriorating day-to-day reality of Palestinian life? Can the world go on distorting truth so that bad agreements, which do not offer much to Palestinians, are not even applied by Israel itself? Can American presidents continue to be indifferent to the daily abuses of Israeli power and never say a word in public expressing the slightest understanding of our Calvary?

Even after the two parties labor to reach an agreement, most often one that fulfills Israeli demands with help from the United States, and even after the agreement is signed, Israel does not always feel bound to the timetable or the content. There is another round of negotiations and the parties end up with another agreement that is even more diluted. There is a sense of apathy in the occupied Palestinian territories and many people have stopped following the news of these events. Past agreements have not borne fruit because they have not addressed the root causes of the conflict, they are not rights based, and do not contain a mechanism to enforce UN resolutions and international law.

The road to peace is not paved with exclusivity or with unending hostility. Rather, it grows out of reconciliation, sharing, and community. Ultimately, there can be no military option for either Palestinians or Israelis.

Lamentations

There is such a great need to tell the truth. For there is no plan, no deal, and no imposed peace process—no matter how powerful—that can succeed without addressing the underlying issues of justice. There are people on all sides—Palestinians, Israelis, internationals—who are trying to tell the truth and are working together to expose the structures of violence, the structures and systems of injustice, which are the very foundation of the conflict.

I have often said that structural and systemic violence is silent. It does not speak, but cries. When it does speak, it often explodes with rage. What we see on television is the violence of the powerless, which is labeled as terrorism.

We do not see or hear the lamentations of the poor. We need to open our hearts and listen, so that we can hear not only the explosions, but also the anguish. Our words echo those of the biblical book of Lamentations.

Remember, O Lord, what has happened to us.

Look at us, and see our disgrace.
Our property is in the hand of strangers;
foreigners are livings in our homes.

Our fathers have been killed by the enemy,
and now our mothers are widows.

We must pay for water we drink;
we must buy the wood we need for fuel.
Driven hard like donkeys or camels,
we are tired, but are allowed no rest.
To get food enough to stay alive,
we went begging in Egypt and Assyria . . .

Our rulers are no better than slaves,
and no one can save us from their power.
Murderers roam through the countryside;
we risk our lives when we look for food.
Hunger has made us burn with fever until our skin is hot as an
oven.

. . . In every . . . village our daughters have been forced to submit.
Our leaders have been taken and hanged;
our elders are shown no respect.
Our young men are forced to grind corn like slaves,
boys go staggering under heavy loads of wood.
The old people no longer sit at the city gate,
and the young people no longer make music.
Happiness had gone out of our lives;
grief has taken the place of our dances.
Nothing is left of all we were proud of . . .
We are sick at our hearts and can hardly see through our tears . . .

But you, O Lord, are king forever and will rule to the end of time.
Why have you abandoned us so long?
Will you ever remember us again?
(Lam. 5:1-6, 8-10, 11b-16a, 17, 19-20, TEV)

If you visit Palestine today, you will hear every Palestinian's cry—man, woman, and child. It is a cry coming from the depths, a cry for justice. These words from the prophets are *our* words. They speak exactly to our situations and our lives. And in the wilderness of occupation, oppression, and exile, we need the prophets more than ever, prophets ancient and modern who proclaim peace with justice, not what the world calls the "peace process."

Christians have been accused both of failing to promote justice in the world and, more seriously, of collaborating with injustice by encouraging the poor and the oppressed to accept their misery patiently and look for abundant rewards in future life. I am very familiar with this particular conception of faith. All it does is remove from our human shoulders our proper task in the present life and induce irresponsibility. For me, faith is a source of power. Faith directs us and activates us to seek justice and love mercy, as the prophet Amos put it. Faith requires a sincere commitment to the healing and reconciliation of the broken world. All of us are aware of Christians and church leaders who seek salvation in words and worship without committing themselves to the quest for a just social order. We have religious leaders who exploit the Bible as they affirm the legitimacy, policies, and conduct of Israel. Without any sense of history, they presume a linkage between biblical Israel and the modern state of Israel.

Affirmations

Of course, the history of condoning injustice in the name of the Bible or some other religious authority is a long one. But, there is a much stronger counterwitness in the Bible and in our religious communities to the bedrock of justice.

Justice is mutual and indivisible. Any lasting peace will have to bring forth true justice for all—Palestinians and Israelis, women and men, Christians, Jews, and Muslims. Peace is for everyone, not just for the powerful. But we cannot have peace if we only continue to recite our litanies of past wrongs and past fears. We must deal with the present. We must look to the future of our children and of all humanity. We must build with new materials, with noncombustibles that will not produce yet more wars.

As a contribution to peace with justice, I offer ten affirmations that are simple and, I hope, universal enough to be a foundation for our common future.

- We affirm the equal value of all races, religions, and peoples. All people reflect the rich plurality of God's creation.

- We affirm that the land belongs to God. Human use of land and waters should release the earth to replenish its life-giving power, protecting its integrity and providing ample space for its creatures. We should resist the dumping of toxic wastes and the unsustainable use of our lands and waters.

- We affirm the claim of every individual upon the resources of the earth as necessities for human survival and recognize the moral obligation of the more fortunate to share resources with those who need them.

- We affirm that all forms of human power and authority are subject to God and accountable to people. This means the right to full participation in resisting oppression, occupation, and power that blocks the processes of transformation toward justice, peace, and the integrity of creation.

- We affirm that male and female are created in the image of God, and that we should resist structures of patriarchy that perpetuate violence against women.

- We affirm that the only possible peace is one based in justice. True peace means every human being dwells in secure relatedness to God, neighbor, nature, and self.

- We affirm the right and responsibility of every individual to use his or her talents for the benefit of the wider community.

- We affirm the search for common values, however differently expressed, in the hope that these values may enable both the individual and the community to overcome greed, thirst for power, and self-seeking.

- We affirm the inseparable relationship between justice, human rights, and peace and will resist systems of society and government that violate human rights and deny the realization of the full potential of individuals and peoples.

- We affirm the presence of a spirit of hope and compassion, available to all, by which our lives may be more whole, more creative, and more harmonious as we draw upon the power that is around us, within us, and within all life.

The issue of peace and justice is complex, overwhelming, and discouraging for many of us. But many of the causes of war and injustice are also within ourselves. For those of us who are lucky, we have three meals a day. We have our jobs, our positions, and our titles. We do not want to be disturbed. We talk about peace. We even have conferences where we listen to many speeches. But, if we are not inwardly transformed, if we still seek power and position, if we are motivated by greed, if we are nationalistic, if we are bound by dogmas and beliefs for which we are willing to die and to destroy others, we cannot have peace in the world. These affirmations are a way of beginning where each of us lives and speaks to the ways of thinking and living that will promote peace.

8

WHAT I OWE MY MUSLIM NEIGHBOR

MY WHOLE LIFE I have lived as an Arab Christian among Muslims. In my early childhood, our town, Ramallah, was more Christian than Muslim, having been settled by seven Christian families long ago. Bireh, our twin town, was mostly Muslim. We always had good relations. There was a mosque in Ramallah and a church in Bireh. My best friends in school were Muslims. Our families and our daily acquaintances were both Muslim and Christian. As the city of Ramallah has grown, so has the mix of Muslims and Christians. Ramallah means the "hill of God." Allah, the name of God, is part of our name and, of course, is part of our daily language as we greet and converse with one another. What we now call "interreligious dialogue" was not separate, conducted around a table. It was just our way of life.

In today's world, I think Islam has been more misunderstood than any other religion. I have to confess that while I knew many, many Muslims, I didn't know that much about Islam myself. I remember when my older son Saleem was in grade four, he came to me and said, "Mother, why in our lessons does it says that Muslims call Abraham the first Muslim when he lived hundreds of years before Muhammed?" I replied, "It must be a mistake in your book." He said, "No, it is written in our history book." I thought something was wrong. I checked with the teacher of Islamic studies and he, smiling, said, "Of course Abraham was a Muslim and so was Jesus." I responded, "How is that?" He smiled again and with great patience and openness said, "Do you know what Islam means? It is the religion of submission to the will, the service, and the commands of God." He went on to explain that the word *Muslim* is a description of a person's relation to God. Whereas most of the names of religions refer to a prophet, a leader, or a nation, Islam describes a person's relationship to God. Anyone who recognizes the greatness of God and surrenders his or her life, in faith, to God is, in this sense, a Muslim.

I think that this was the first time that I really considered what the words *Islam* and *Muslim* meant in spiritual terms. I have lived all my life in a country where Muslims are a majority of the population. My native language is Arabic. My culture is part of the Islamic culture, so this should have been clear to me all along. Thankfully, this moment of discovery helped me stand outside myself and the culture that had shaped me and begin to view things differently. Not only did I see Islam differently—as an action, a relationship, a way of living in relation to God—but I also learned something more about my own faith. This experience heightened my awareness of my own faith as a relationship, as living human life in concordance with God's will. It made me ponder deeply. Too often, we have presented each other's religion in a very false light, sometimes simply because of our ignorance. I began to think more about Christianity and Islam together, asking not only what we can learn about one another, but what we learn from each other about God and our relationship with God.

What have I learned from my Muslim neighbors? Islam affirms a meeting between God, as God is, and human beings, as they are. That is to say, God is envisaged, not as God is manifest in a particular way or at a particular time, but independent of history. God as God is: the One whose very nature creates and reveals. Human as human is: the created one endowed with intelligence and will, capable of choosing that which leads one to God.

This was a help to me and also a relief. Throughout my life the one image of God that had been communicated to me was that which came from biblical history—active, involved, speaking, judging, chastising, and loving. Historical images tend to be preserved as truth and the actions and patterns of moral behavior that resulted from God's revelation in the particular circumstances of the past become the norms for succeeding generations. You may say, "And why not?" I too asked myself this question. Why not? Because God is living and God's will is to be discerned afresh each moment in the changing circumstances of life. God is related dynamically to the present. Because the present is never exactly like the past, the precise meaning of God for us can be known only in the present. Images of God may come from the past, but the reality of God is in the present.

Prayer

Standing under God's gracious sky, Muslims can at any moment lift their heads directly into the Divine Presence to receive both strength and guidance for the living of their days. They have such ready access to the Divine because nothing stands between the person and Allah. As the Qur'an puts it,

> Is he not closer than the vein of thy neck?
> Thou needest not raise thy voice, for He knoweth
> the secret whisper and what is yet more hidden.
> He knows what is in the land and in the sea.[1]

I learned from my neighbors why prayer is one of the pillars of Islam. Christians pray, too, but for Muslims there is a regularity, a constancy, in prayer. One basic reason for prayer is to keep one's life in perspective. Humans are weak and apt to place themselves at the center of their own universe. People too readily forget that they are creatures and not the Creator. Prayer five times a day is a constant reminder of the Creator and of one's submission to the will of God, the *ilah*. The Arabic word *ilah* means *maabood*, or object of worship, which is derived from *abd*, slave or servant. *Ibadat*, worship, which is the abstract noun from *abd*, does not merely imply ritual worship; it means a life of continuous service and unremitting obedience. To wait upon a person in service, to bow in reverence, to acknowledge God's reign, to exert oneself in obedience to God's commands—these are the real implications of the term *ibadat*. A person's true object of worship can only be the One to whom he or she is related in this way.

Five times a day, then, the object of worship is *El Rab*. What is the meaning of *rab*? This Arabic word means "one who nourishes." Since our moral consciousness tells us that the one who nourishes, sustains, and provides for us has a strong claim on our allegiance, the word *rab* is also used in the sense of master or owner. A person's *rab* is the one whom he or she regards as nourisher and patron, from whom he or she expects favor and toward whom he or she feels obligations, whose displeasure is considered to be harmful to one's life and happiness, and whom one follows and obeys. Keeping in view the meaning of these two words, *ilah* and *rab*, we may decide who it is that may rightfully claim to be a human's *ilah* and *rab* and who may therefore demand one's service and worship. Trees, stones, rivers, the sun, the moon—none of these can properly lay claims to such worship. It is only humans who sometimes falsely make such an assertion of godliness in relation to their fellow human beings. What a presumption!

The words, "I acknowledge no God but you alone," repeated in the daily prayers, serve to remind the worshiper that God is great and that God alone is to be worshiped and served—and not earthly rulers or kings, not whatever the world offers in status and wealth.

Human beings are being created in the image of God and are distinguished from other creatures by their superior intelligence, their free will, and the gift of speech. Speech is communication with God and is essentially prayer and invocation. This is why the Arabic language is a religious language, thoroughly saturated with the name of God.

Pillars of Faith

Prayer is the first of the five pillars of Islam and it is by far the most visible throughout the Muslim world because of its regularity and unabashed public practice. Less visible, but equally important, is the disposition of the heart that goes with prayer, *the affirmation of faith*. Perhaps the one doctrine of Islam is the affirmation of the *shahadah*: "There is no God but God and Mohammed is His prophet." The first line declares that God alone is and that all things are dependent upon Him. Many of the phrases we use in the Arabic language express this principle, "Verily we are God's and unto Him we return" and "In the name of God, the infinitely Good, the ever Merciful." There is nothing more central in Islam than the affirmation of God's oneness, what Muslims refer to as the doctrine of *tawhid*.

Islam contributed much to the concept of the universality of God. Christianity and Judaism are more exclusive, qualifying the universality of God with the particularity of peoplehood or divine revelation. For the Muslim, God is truly universal. God shares the Godhead with no one, and God has no chosen people. Islam abolished the organized priesthood, the sacraments, and all the ceremonials that come between God and the worshiper.

I have often asked Muslim friends about the way in which Islam counsels people to live. They all reply that Islam teaches them to walk in "the straight path." This phrase comes from the opening Surah of the Qur'an itself and is recited by every practicing Muslim five times a day.

> Praise belongs to God, Lord of the Worlds,
> The Compassionate, the Merciful
> King of the Day of Judgment,
> 'Tis Thee we worship and Thee we ask for help.
> Guide us in the straight path, the path of these
> You have favored, not the path of those who incur
> Thine anger, nor of those who go astray.
> (Qur'an 1, The Fatiha)

Muslims feel that Islam has a clarity, an order, a precision that is in sharp contrast to the shifting, relative, uncertain, "at sea" quality of much of modern life.

Fasting is another pillar of Islam—specifically, the observance of fasting during the month of Ramadan. Men and women, young and old, fast during this month from daybreak to sunset without food or drink. I have tried to fast to find out how my students and fellow teachers experienced the fasting of this month. To tell the truth, I found it too difficult. So much self-discipline is required that the person who can endure it will have less difficulty controlling his or her appetite at other times. Fasting also induces compassion. Only those who have been hungry can know what hunger means. Compassion, self-control, faithfulness, and peace are all qualities strengthened during Ramadan.

Another pillar of Islam that has much to teach us is *pilgrimage.* The basic purpose of the yearly pilgrimage to Mecca is to increase the pilgrim's devotion to God and to God's revealed will, but the practice has many other beneficial effects as well. It is a reminder of the equality between people. All distinctions of rank disappear; prince and pauper stand before God in their undivided humanity. Pilgrimage also provides a useful service in international affairs. It brings together people from various countries, demonstrating that they have in common a loyalty that transcends the loyalties of warring nations. Pilgrims learn firsthand about their brothers and sisters in other lands and return to their own with better understanding of one another. Islam, according to my Muslim friends, not only stresses racial equality, but makes it evident. Abraham's second wife, Hagar, they say, was black. So was one of Muhammad's wives, and so was his first muezzin who was charged with offering the call to prayer.

In addition there is much to learn from the *economic regulations* that are also a pillar of Islam. The obligation to pay *zakat,* an annual and voluntary tax for the well-being of the whole community, especially the poor, enables Muslims to make their wider understanding of community a reality. Of course, among so many Palestinians, of whom almost 60 percent live below the poverty line on less than two dollars a day, the offering of *zakat* is a difficult obligation to fulfill.

Islam insists that all of human life—from the habits of daily life to matters of ethics, law, and government—should be related to God. For Muslims anything that touches any part of their lives, touches religion. Traditionally, an Islamic government cannot be secular, if by that we mean anti-religious. But that does not mean an Islamic government cannot be democratic.

The Stereotypes

What about women and the status of women in Islam? It is often thought, especially in the West, that Islam is oppressive for women. There is no doubt that women and men have traditionally different roles in our part of the Muslim world, but I have learned that, historically, Islam in fact improved the status of women from what it had been in pre-Islamic Arabia. Given the experience of Christian women in the churches through the ages, it is my sense that the role and image of women in our two traditions is a topic that invites our joint investigation. Both traditions have had a very mixed record.

What about the use of force? The Western stereotype of a Muslim is that of a man marching with a sword. I admit that the Qur'an does not counsel turning the other cheek or pacifism, but it does teach forgiveness and the returning of good for evil, and these are very different from resisting evil only with force. While outsiders have seen Islam as the religion of the sword, spread and upheld by the sword, we have to ask whether the accounts of God's people in the Old Testament don't also display a warrior God. And how about Christianity? Christians, too, made use of the sword from the time of Constantine in the fourth century onwards. Our Muslim friends ask, "Who was it who preached the Crusades in the name of the 'Prince of Peace?'" The Crusades offer a terrible testimony to Christianity as a religion of the sword. And, even today, military hardware in the so-called Christian West is produced in horrifying quantities. Our Muslim friends ask, "Who was it who made and first used the atomic bomb?" Muslims consider the record of the Christian West much more violent than their own, as well as the record of Israel, a Jewish state.

Confronting the stereotypes of Islam through the eyes of my Muslim neighbors has made me more aware of the progressive and reactionary forms of expression that are part of every religious tradition. On the one hand, narrow, chauvinistic, and violent use and abuse of religion has entered into and shaped almost every major conflict and crisis in the world today. There is self-serving narrowness, militant chauvinism, and patriarchy in every religious tradition. On the other side, there are movements in the churches as well as among Jewish, Muslim, and Buddhist activists that aim to resist and transform the structures that keep so much of the human race oppressed and in poverty. There are activist, feminist, reform, and peace movements in every tradition. When people speak about fundamentalists and mean "Muslim fanatics," it is important not to forget that there are right-wing religionists everywhere, and not least in Palestine and Israel. That does not relieve us of the obligation to oppose them, but we must not succumb to the illusion that the fanatics are all in someone else's camp.

Muslim-Christian Relations

Many people think that when one becomes more aware, more appreciative, and more understanding of the contributions of another religious tradition, one is watering down his or her own religion. This is not so in my experience. Whether we succeed or fail in understanding our Muslim neighbors, we do so as Christians. Our Christian convictions are of the utmost importance in the work of relating to people. My work and life in a pluralistic society has challenged me to understand the fullness of Christ. But my understanding of God would be much more limited if I had lived in isolation from the other people, from my Muslim neighbors.

There have been varied and complex crises in Christian-Muslim relations. From the standpoint of the Middle East, we often feel that behind these crises lurks the pervasive influence of the West, with its mixture of political and material power, its religious intolerance, and at the same time its penetrating influence. Over the decades, the influence of the West has often had the effect of detaching the Muslim from his or her own supreme loyalty to the demands of God. Of course, I recognize that there have been tensions for over a thousand years between Muslim and Christian groups and that there have been faults and aggressions on both sides, but surely our path today is to try to understand the dark shadow that has been cast everywhere by the colonialism and the wanton aggressiveness, as they see it, of the Christian West.

We Christians have been more severe in our attitude toward Islam than we are toward ourselves. If, on the other hand, we begin with a criticism of ourselves and work toward a better attitude toward Muslims, this may bring them to a better and healthier understanding of Christianity, not as monolithic, but as complex and self-critical. We shall realize that differences, problems, and difficulties are not in reality "religious" but that, rather, religion is too often used to conceal other issues, as for example, in Northern Ireland where the bloodshed is not primarily about forms of Christianity, but about patterns of domination and power.

A mutual and constructive dialogue of Muslims and Christians is beginning in many places today. When Christians try to read some of the basic prayers repeated daily by Muslims they find that the Gospel and Islam are concerned with similar things—the reality, the oneness, and the sovereignty of God, God's revelation to humankind, human responsibility for ethical choice, God's call to submission and obedience, and God's justice and mercy. Here we find all the elements needed for a fruitful dialogue. Discovering common ideals will free us from the bonds of slavery to earthly and material powers. Muslims and Christians have a real mission together—to deliver people from the injustice of slavery, from false gods, and from the tyranny of exploitation of the weaker by the stronger. Therefore, I believe dialogue is a fundamental part of Christian service and witness within community.

In dialogue, we respond to the command to "Love God and your neighbor as yourself." This love sets us free to be open to the faiths of others, to risk, to trust, and to be vulnerable. This love evokes in us an attitude of real humility toward all people since we know that we, together with all our brothers and sisters, have fallen short of the community that God intends.

9

SOLIDARITY WITH WOMEN

ONE OF THE BEAUTIFUL POSTERS made by Palestinians for the Beijing Women's Conference in 1995 is a painting of women walking, taking long strides, while looking up into the horizon. They don't seem to be bent down by their bodies' pain, anxiety, and hurt, for they have started their journey to affirm life by upholding the ideals written in Arabic on the poster: justice, equality, and freedom.

As Palestinians and as women our struggle to achieve these ideals continues today. It has been a long struggle, waged on so many fronts. It has been a long walk, and a long road to freedom still lies ahead. On the way, we often get tired, confused, and frustrated; we sometimes lose direction; we find ourselves at an impasse or headed down a one-way or a no-entry or even a dead-end. But this has not discouraged us or made us give up our journey with others and for others. In fact, the difficulties of our journey have made the issues of the struggle even clearer and have revealed to us the interconnectedness of unjust structures, the web of oppression, and the various struggles for liberation.

The call for liberation is heard everywhere, by women and by many others. It is not an empty slogan or a liturgical anthem. Rather, it is a cry, a cry from the heart, a cry out of humiliation and oppression, a cry for a new future—beginning now.

Will our religious structures or our churches hear this cry for liberation? It was two decades ago, in January 1987, that the Central Committee of the World Council of Churches designated the years 1988 to 1998 as the Ecumenical Decade of Churches in Solidarity with Women. The decision to highlight this issue for a ten-year period was in response to deep and growing concerns from all over the world about the situation of women in societies and churches.

The aims of the Decade were:

1. To empower women to challenge oppressive structures in the global community, their country, and their church;

2. To affirm in shared leadership and decision making, theology and spirituality, the decisive contribution women are already making in churches and communities;

3. To give visibility to women's perspectives and actions in the struggle for justice, peace, and the integrity of creation;

4. To enable churches to free themselves from teachings and practices that discriminate against women;

5. To encourage churches to take action in solidarity with women.

Many people had hoped that the UN Decade and the Churches' Decade in Solidarity with Women would lead to the radical transformation of our societies and of the situation of women who suffer from poverty, economic exploitation, sexism, racism, and violence. However, the sad truth is that not much changed during those ten years. Indeed, today many women face more difficult conditions than they did fifteen or twenty years ago.

And yet there have been milestones along the way that have made a difference in our collective understanding. For example, women urged their churches to respond to the Jubilee Call to break the stranglehold of debt with a policy of debt forgiveness. Just as the biblical jubilee (Lev.

25:10) restored the community by freeing those enslaved by crushing debts, so the modern Jubilee movement, an alliance of some eighty religious denominations and human rights groups, insists on a new jubilee to cancel the enslaving debt of poor countries. The aim of the Jubilee movement is to address the social, political, and ecological costs of the cycle of debt, to offer a fresh start for the poor, and to establish a just global order by reordering the priorities of wealthy nations. These issues are women's issues.

The biblical jubilee is not simply the search for justice. It is an attempt to provide a comprehensive vision of a social and economic order in which justice is an essential element. Central to the understanding of the biblical jubilee is the self-limitation of power exercised through the control over land, capital, labor, and women. The jubilee indicates a new beginning, and a chance to change economic, social, political, and cultural life so that order might be restored to persons, so that creation and property might be restored to their rightful condition, so that a door might be opened to the future.

The Jubilee movement's call focused on the millennium, but its importance is ongoing. It is a pivotal alternative to the prevailing order of exclusion and marginalization. It is the celebration of life-centered values in the midst of despair.

The Struggle for Justice Is One Struggle

Over the years I have learned that the struggle for justice is one struggle, involving women and men, people of all nations, and people of all religious traditions. We defend human rights and promote justice in one place on behalf of people everywhere. Our global and local responsibilities are related. Global issues have a local face, and local issues have global connections. The kinship we form as we cultivate an understanding of our global and local relatedness has become the prototype of a new community. It is a community that knows no national, racial, or gender/sexual boundaries.

For me, it has been the women's movement for liberation, both locally and globally, that has most deeply touched me and forced me to change. Women's roles and status lie at the heart of every society. Girl babies may not be buried alive, as was the practice deep in the past, but even now parents in many countries welcome a baby boy more enthusiastically than a girl. We have so much work to do simply to unlearn what we have learned and to look out from different windows. It is not always that simple. Often I see that women themselves reinforce structures of injustice in the way they educate and raise their families. Often women use their own power to dominate and coerce, rather than utilizing the resources of co-powering and cooperation. Coercive power is oppressive and marginalizes others from the centers of decision making. Power can be used in a constructive way, however, so that everyone has the power to act justly, to control their own lives, and to influence their own communities.

Another difficulty of the women's movement is that certain trends are assumed to be somehow global. For example, women who choose to be mothers and take care of the family may be judged as if their vocation and self-worth is less than that of professional women. No woman should impose on others her choices, lifestyle, or values; rather, we should struggle so that women will have equal opportunities with men and the freedom to choose where to invest their energies.

Women in different paths of our society might be struggling to change different things at different times. The overworked woman, contending with hunger and inadequate living conditions, is unlikely to be worried about sexist language, but this fact does not mean that one issue is more important than another. All of us are on this journey for freedom with others and for others, so rather than discrediting each others' struggles, we must join hands, enrich, and inspire one another to bring about a true community where justice and righteousness reign. And righteousness means right relationships, rather than transferring power and privilege from one group to another. No one is free until we are all free.

On this journey, struggling to transform our societies and ourselves, we often experience fatigue and we may become burned-out unless we are sustained by a commitment and a spirituality that is deeper than the ethics of revolution alone. The act of recovering our source, the realization that we are created in the image of God, is, for women, a redemptive act. It is to reclaim our lost wholeness and our sense of self-worth.

Freedom is not a new theme in Christian theology. The gospel itself is a message of liberation in Jesus Christ. It is good news to all people in every situation and in every place of internal and external oppression. The situations may vary but all of us want to be alive and free. The struggle begins in a woman's own heart, mind, and actions as she learns to be pro-woman. But it must stretch around the world to all people—men, women, and children who are looking for freedom to shape their own futures and participate in the search for what it means to be children of God. The yearning for freedom and the spiritual affirmation of liberation is not just a Christian theme. It is part of the spiritual realization of people in every religious tradition.

The Palestinian Reality

Most of the media images of Palestinians are of men and boys by the hundreds in the streets in Gaza, whether at demonstrations or funerals. And, of course, virtually every funeral is also demonstration. But when there is gunfire, when there are deaths, when there are funerals, women are involved. They do not leave the house and stream through the streets, but women are still holding up half the sky. Much of the work of women is invisible, especially in the eye of the media.

The women of Palestine are often referred to as the "glue of our society." We are the ones who hold our families together, while our husbands, brothers, and sons are in prison, deported, wounded, or killed, or when they have migrated for economic or political reasons. Yet, as in all societies, we Palestinian women have been cast into roles that have kept us subservient and out of critical decision-making circles. In the national liberation movement, women's work has not been considered equal to men's work. In the churches, the ministries of women have been considered less important than those of men. Even though we are the "glue" of society, the contributions of women have been considered less important than those of men. Even though, as women in Palestine, we are full participants in our national struggle, we are not fully recognized as part of the decision-making bodies.

So as a Palestinian woman, I find myself struggling on two fronts. Palestinian women must work for liberation on the national front while, at the same time, working for liberation as women on the societal level. We have to struggle to free ourselves from hierarchy and from the male-dominated structures of our society.

The first intifada (1987–1993) began to change some attitudes, but we still have a long way to go. Today women are organizing at the grassroots level and are beginning to connect the national struggle with the women's struggle for liberation. Today, there are many Palestinian women who are leading NGOs (nongovernmental organizations).

As presiding clerk of the Quakers, I am the only woman heading a religious organization engaged in the Middle East resistance and non-violent action of Palestinian women. Even so, we Palestinian women live and work in a very traditional society where the dos and don'ts for women are made very clear. Often our effectiveness in leadership depends on how well we follow the expectations of our own people. If we don't meet their expectations, our work may not be validated or even taken seriously. Unfortunately, most people cannot look beyond the superficial, so if I hope to be effective, I have to be careful not to lose the respect of the community. I constantly live life in my traditional society on the one hand and in the ever-changing world on the other hand.

Let me give you one simple, personal example of this tension. When people learned that I was involved in the World Council of Churches ecumenical movement, they used to react in several different ways. Some were amused that someone like me had a role in a worldwide movement; some were simply scornful that I would take time away from my responsibilities to travel to India or Canada; and some were embarrassingly deferential.

I tried to explain that I am as concerned with the human condition in general as I am with our own specific conflicts that often represent only the tip of a pyramid of anguish and violence. I would say that I am concerned with all the pain and confusion that impedes our human unfolding and fulfillment. My own understanding of the ecumenical movement is that it is a movement of the Spirit, a movement of Christians throughout the world that unites and reconciles us. The Spirit transforms us into a caring and sharing people, breaking down the walls that separate us. The Spirit empowers us in our struggle for justice and peace. Some people say that your faith or your spirituality is your own private affair. I completely disagree, for spirituality includes all the dimensions of human, personal, and societal living. All these combine to make human life human—the measure of the fullness of God's gift.

The human family is in crisis whenever communities and persons, including women, experience despair, hopelessness, alienation, violation, and exploitation. Many systems are interconnected, including our religious, economic, social, political, military, transportation, communication, education, and value systems. Some of these values must be altered when individuals and institutions become aware of the limits of their own culture and their own church contexts and become involved in a movement based on global perspectives and engaged in wider change.

As co-partners in the struggle for justice, women are critically involved in a mostly nonviolent struggle. We continue to work, support, and build for a new future, a future time in which, through our liberation, all of the Middle East, and all of humanity, would be liberated. It is this hope that inspires us and leads us. And it is this hope that allows us to see the image of God in everyone. It is this hope that will turn the sufferings into a new dawn for all humanity.

The Biblical Women of Palestine: Biblical Teachings and Hard Realities

For Palestinian Christian women, the liberating words, teachings, and actions of Jesus in relation to women become an inspiration and a guide for us in our struggle for the liberation of our own people and for humanity, both on the political level as well as on the social level. There are many women, in a sense our own ancestors, depicted in the New Testament. Who were they? What were their self-images? How did Jesus respond to each of them?

My own life experience leads me to begin with a recollection of the Samaritan woman who met Jesus at the well (John 4:1-42), a well just an hour north of Ramallah, the place where I grew up and still live. She came in the heat of the day, we are told, because her social position did not allow her to join the other women who drew water in the cool of the morning. She was taken aback by Jesus' request for a drink, indeed by Jesus' engagement with her at all. Clearly, her self-image was not a positive one. We learn that she had had five husbands and was now living with a man who was not her husband. But Jesus, knowing all this, looked beyond it and accepted her ministry to him—a drink of water. Moreover, in forgiving her, he opened to her new possibilities for living.

Sometimes, as Palestinian women, we feel the burden of the Samaritan woman in relation to her family and her society. We have so many things with which to deal in our society while, at the same time, the hierarchical structure of our church and of our whole culture hinders our growth and limits our involvement. The expectations imposed upon us by family and friends, moreover, become an overwhelming burden as we seek to be faithful to God's calling. We, too, are hauling water in the heat of the day, and we yearn for a teaching that allays our deep spiritual thirst.

As a Palestinian woman, I also find much to which I can relate in the story of Mary and Martha (Luke 10:38-42). The story deals with the relationship between two sisters, and, of course, family relationships are particularly important to us Arabs. They form the very basis of our society. Then the story reminds us of the gifts that are given to all of us and of the roles we all play. Jesus reminds us that each of us is unique and, no matter who we are or what we do, we must each be concerned with God's work and the Household of Life. Martha is worried about the tasks of the household, while Mary sits at the feet of Jesus. It is not easy in a society where women are expected to do all the housework and family tasks. If we wish to be involved in other work—work in the church or work in the society—it must be done in addition to the work expected of us at home.

The story of Martha and Mary points to the ongoing tension to which we can all relate, that between contemplation and activity. Activity without contemplation is empty and contemplation without activity is dead. Conventionally, Mary is understood to be a pious and prayerful contemplative, while Martha is active, but less prayerful. Origen read Jesus' rebuke of Martha as justifying his own view of the subordination of the active life to the contemplative. Augustine showed a balance between the two drives, one to contemplation and the other to active service. The Cistercians, too, commended a combination of Martha and Mary. Among the mendicant friars, Francis had both types live together and encouraged them to exchange roles, while Aquinas insisted that Mary could not have the best portion unless she shared the fruits of her contemplation.

Meister Eckhart, the thirteenth-century Dominican mystic, went even further. For him it is Martha who is the more mature. The religious life of his period had quite enough "Marys" who were so caught up in their own mortifications that they had not the freedom to follow God spontaneously, or respond to the needs of the neighbor. Martha, in Eckhart's view, was more mature than Mary, in that she had learned from experience to be both active and in essential communion with Christ. She was not complaining of Mary to Jesus, as much as trying to ensure that Mary would not remain stuck in the pleasant feeling of intimacy with Jesus. Jesus, for his part, was not putting Martha in her place, but was assuring her that Mary would eventually reach her full potential, by being like Martha. It was only later when she had heard of Jesus' ascension and had received the Holy Spirit that Mary learned to serve, by crossing the sea, preaching, teaching, and serving the disciples.

I am rather taken by Eckhart's reading of Luke's account. Yet, a quick glance at some of the most recent commentaries on Luke discovers nothing of Eckhart's insight on this point. Perhaps the fear of having to become active, rather than mere keyboard exponents of the Word, prevents some from such a reading of the text.

The story of the woman who wipes Jesus' feet with her tears and her ointment occurs in all four Gospels and, indeed, it is sometimes said to be Mary who anoints Jesus this way. The story is all too often misinterpreted. Instead of focusing on the ministry and the intentions of the woman, interpreters tend to focus on her impurity or wastefulness. But Jesus does not do this. Rather, he accepts her ministry, forgives her sins, and focuses on her intention. It was a radical position for a man to take in those days!

I have grown up in a culture that often imposes certain traditional cultural values through which women are allotted a second-class place. This secondary place for women is frequently given biblical approval by the use of Ephesians 5 in the context of marriage services. As it is used in the liturgy the text appears to foster in wives an attitude of submission to their husbands that is offensive to the egalitarianism which one looks for between the sexes. For that reason the text is offensive.

But, on this occasion, one should not blame Paul, but his careless translators. The act of removing the text from its context, and its common translation distorts what is in the mind of the writer of Ephesians. This can be seen readily if one goes back to verse 15 of chapter 5. In that way it reads as follows:

> Therefore [in sum, or, in other words], watch carefully how you behave—not as unwise people but as wise ones—redeeming the time, for the days are evil. For that very reason do not be senseless, but understand what is the will of the Lord. And do not get drunk with wine—that is profligacy—but be filled in spirit talking to one another in psalms, and hymns, and spiritual songs, singing and making music to the Lord in your hearts giving thanks to God the father, always on behalf of all in the name of our Lord Jesus Christ, being subordinate to one another out of reverence for Christ, wives to your own husbands as to the Lord, for the husband is the head of the wife, as Christ is head of the church . . . . (Eph. 5:15-23; my translation)

The first surprise is that the phrase "be subject to" or "subordinate to" does not occur between "wives" and "your husbands" in the Greek, although translators insist on supplying it in their translations. The

Revised Standard Version reads, "Wives, be subject to your husbands, as to the Lord," and the New Jerusalem Bible has, "Wives should be subject to their husbands as to the Lord." But I think it is altogether improper to supply the words "be subject to" in this place, since its inclusion appears to reduce the previous statement of *mutual submission* of all the members of the community to the one example of wives in relation to their husbands.[1]

The effect of the mistranslation in the Ephesians text is highlighted when the text of the letter is broken at verse 22 ("Wives, be subject to your husbands as you are to the Lord") for whatever reason, liturgical or otherwise. It then appears that "being subject to" is an injunction only to wives with respect to their husbands, when in fact the text makes it clear that "being subordinate to" is a disposition that the writer expects of each member of the community with respect to all others.

Nevertheless, this biblical passage as it is used in the liturgy, and in the marriage rite in particular, confirms hierarchical domination in the marriage relationship. The problem is not only with the interpretation of the text, but also with the way in which many understand the Bible as holding all the authority of the word of God. But I believe the word of God is much more than that. The Bible is a history of people's experiences of God and how these people perceived God, and yet it does not contain the whole reality of God.

Maybe the letter to the Ephesians could be an achievement or an improvement in a certain historical and cultural context when relationships were not regulated and men had many wives. But this cannot be valid today. Repeating this text at all marriage ceremonies in my country confirms the subordination of women. One wonders what the effect might be if we did not so seriously misrepresent the author of the text. Yet, for me, hope to overcome the powers of darkness to establish peace may be found elsewhere in Ephesians. Indeed, according to Paul we are liberated from sin and division and united in the Spirit (Eph. 4:4).

I perceive Christ as the inward teacher, cleansing men and women of sin and bringing them back to their original state where they were equally created in the image of God as partners and helpmates. For me, the equality of women in ministry, in the business of the church, and in marriage is essential if we are to have harmonious relationships. In a community without dominance, there is no need for war, for as Paul says, "There is no longer Jew or Greek, there is no longer slave or free, there is no longer male and female; for all of you are one in Christ Jesus" (Gal. 3:28). Marriage within the holy community should therefore take on a whole different meaning than in our cultures. It must be a marriage of equals, of mutual support, so that each partner is free to follow the leadings of the Holy Spirit.

While generations of religious people have derived profit and pleasure from the retelling of biblical stories, victims of oppression—including women and the Palestinians—pose fundamental moral questions that relate to one's understanding of the nature of God, of God's dealings with humankind, and of human behavior. Many of these biblical traditions have been deployed in support of violent oppressive behavior in a wide variety of contexts. In the spirit of contemporary moral discourse, it is a matter of grave concern that the Bible was used and is still used by many as a tool of colonialism, oppression, and domination of women. But things are changing.

10

NEIGHBORS

You yourselves used to be in the darkness, but since you have become the Lord's people, you are in the light. So you must live like people who belong to the light, for it is the light that brings a rich harvest of every kind of goodness, righteousness, and truth.—Eph. 5:8-9 (TEV)

I WANT TO TAKE YOU ON A TRIP to my hometown, Ramallah. It is 10:30 in the morning and I am sitting in my bright living room overlooking the garden in the courtyard. Facing me on the table is an arrangement of golden orange and yellow marigolds. On another table is a lovely arrangement of daffodils, tulips, and hyacinth, raised and picked by my mother and aunt and waiting for my son to collect them for his birthday today. These flowers have come out of the darkness of the earth, which is itself the shadow of the divine darkness from which all things come. They came out of the darkness into the light of the world, radiant with its brightness and reflecting its glory.

In another corner of the room there is a green plant with all the leaves turning toward the light. No matter how I turn the pot, the leaves direct themselves to the light.

Facing me above the fireplace is a framed photograph of the opening prayer of the Qur'an that I received as a gift from Hartford

Seminary in America. A section of the prayer reads: "Lead me, God, to the right path." Around the room are photographs of my children and their spouses, photographs of my grandchildren, paintings of birds from Mexico and Egypt, beautiful handicrafts from Africa, Palestinian embroidery and glasswork, and many reminders of friends in different parts of the world.

As I look out on this world of things around me—each one separated in space, each moving in time—all is one, united in a simple vision of being. I use images to help me turn my mind toward the Light and allow the Light itself to enlighten me. Perhaps this room is like the white light of the sun in which all the colors of the rainbow are present, while each retains its distinctive character. So it is with the world in which we live as well. Perhaps the room is like a symphony in which all the notes are heard in a single perfect harmony, but in which each has its own particular time and place. Or going deeper, perhaps this room is like a community of persons, connected through time and space by the strong strands of love through which each understands the other and is somehow connected with the other.

On one of the shelves of this spacious room is a framed painting of a beautiful child carrying a lantern. The child has a halo of light around his head. I think the person in the painting is one artist's idea of Jesus.

Next to the painting is written:

My dear Jean,
There is nothing to fear
Because Jesus is near.
His love is the light
That makes all things come right.
May Jesus be your light throughout your life.

Your aunt,
Sr. Celestin Mikhail
Bethlehem, 8.9.1955

My aunt, Sister Celestin, a Roman Catholic sister, once painted this on one page in my autograph book. In 1968, I decided to have it framed. As I think of my aunt and my family and the countless persons from all corners of the earth and all from different backgrounds, nations, religions, and professions who were here in my living room, I am constantly reminded that each human being is a focus of the Divine Light which shines within all equally, each receiving it according to his or her own capacity.

No two souls are the same, and the experience of each is unique. It is as though one Divine Light is received into each of us, but every one of us is reflecting it in his or her own way and breaking it up into many colors. Each is a unique reflection of the one Light.

Where does sin and evil come into the picture? Why is there so much darkness, injustice, and oppression in our world? Why is it so difficult to see the Divine Light in others? Throughout my life, I have longed to find answers to this question, and I have often turned to the words of the seventeenth-century English Quaker James Nayler to provide some guidance, though his time was so different from our own. Its archaic language makes me slow down and think carefully:

> As thou becomest faithful there to, thou wilt feel the fruit of that Holy one springing in thee, moving to be brought forth in thee, towards God and man, which if thou willingly serve in its smallest notion, it will be increased, but if thou quench it in its movings, and refuse to bring it forth, it will wither and die in thee, not being exercised. And it is like gentleness, meekness, patience, and all other virtues which are of a springing and spreading nature where they are not quenched, and daily increase with using. But if thou will not give up for His name's sake, but would hold the treasure, and escape the reproach, it will be taken from thee. What a glory to see peace shine in the midst of war. Love in the midst of hatred. Righteous judgement in the midst of wickedness. Innocency in the midst of violence and oppression. As a lily among thorns so is that of God amongst the people of the world.[1]

Here it is important to know that Friends or Quakers have used different phrases to mean the same thing. For instance, the "light within," is also called the "inner light," the "inward light," the "light of Christ," "Christ within," the "seed," or "that of God in every person." How do we nurture those virtues that, as he puts it, are "of a springing and spreading nature" so they will not wither?

For Friends, the inward light is the light of Christ within. The inner light is not just the light of conscience or reason, your light and my light. It is Divine Light, the light of God. Many individuals and religious groups stop here and forget the fundamental part of Quaker testimony—that God's light shines in the heart of everyone, young and old, good and evil, Christian, Jew, and Muslim. When I as a Christian center on Christ, I become more and more open to the universal light, rather than becoming more and more exclusive. I cannot feel superior and assume that our light is the only light. The light did not come from ourselves. When we make ourselves the judge and master, we fall into the great illusion we call sin. This is what is happening in all of us. Each becomes centered on herself or himself, in conflict with the neighbor, forgetting the light we share with all humanity, with all creatures. Sin is the failure of love—a failure to respond to the movement of grace that is ever drawing us out of ourselves into the divine life, into the light.

Light cannot be thought of apart from darkness and we are committed to one as to the other. The light shines in the darkness. One without the other has no meaning. Recognition of the darkness in ourselves and in others, individually and collectively, comes as we grow in awareness of the reality of God and water those spring and spreading intimations within.

I have taken you home to my living room. I shared with you the light of beauty, of awareness, of interconnectedness, of sharing, of equality and universality. This same light has also exposed what is evil in our world—the violence, destruction, poverty, denial of basic human rights, and injustice.

Who Is My Neighbor?

Recognizing that the light is not ours alone, we understand that it opens us to the light of others. As a Christian, Palestinian, and Arab, native of the Holy Land, I have lived all my life in a culture where the law of neighborhood is of great importance and influence. It takes rank after family life with regard to the number and authority of the customs created and regulated by it. Neighborhood is not an occasional community feeling, but a constant necessity of our social life. Our life cannot be understood apart from this law of neighborhood.

But who *is* my neighbor and what does this word mean? This, of course, was the question that the rich young man who asked Jesus, "What must I do to inherit eternal life?" And Jesus responded with the great commandments, "Love God and love your neighbor as yourself." Good enough, but the young man was not satisfied. "Who is my neighbor?" he asked. Jesus responded with the story of the man who had been beaten up by thieves and lay by the side of the road. Many people passed by, too busy to attend, including priests who should have cared. The one who stopped to tend to him and to see that he received care was a Samaritan, a foreigner, not even one of his co-religionists. He was the real neighbor.

The Arabic word for neighbor, *saken karib*, means the inhabitant nearby and the friend. My neighbor therefore is a person who is entrusted to me, who is safe in my company. If a person is asking to be my neighbor, he or she is crying for help, asking for refuge and safety. If I am a neighbor to those who are "inhabitants nearby," it means I am with them in their troubles, rescue them from their difficulties. This is exactly what the noun, verb, and adjective of "neighbor" in Arabic mean.

Who were my neighbors along the journey of my life? When I was a child, I spent most of my time with my neighbors, young and old. They lived nearby and some of them were also relatives. We played together, went to the fields to pick grapes and olives together, and went to church together. We helped each other in our housework, cooking, embroidery, and even schoolwork. We borrowed from each other valuables for hospitality on special occasions. We borrowed bread, flour, matches, and kitchen utensils in emergencies. Our domestic life was touched at every point by our neighbors.

As the Bible references indicate, neighborhood is an institution of high social value with privileges to be enjoyed and duties to be discharged. My neighbors were helpful, sincere, and intimate. Over the years, the bonds with many of them have been stronger than those with relatives, which proved to me how much truth lies in the proverb, "Better is a neighbor that is near than a brother who is far away."

I must say my neighbors obeyed the commandment, "Thou shalt love your neighbor." As a child, I felt loved by every one of them. I always felt secure, accepted, and encouraged in every way. When I got sick, my grandmother used to say that my illness was a result of the loving eyes of my neighbors. I should not be loved so much. I was overwhelmed with love, and that love helped me to see the meaning of religious faith in ordinary, daily human experience. In seeking to respond to this love, I found a sense of meaning and purpose for my life. Each stage of my life offered fresh opportunities, questions, challenges, and temptations. When I was married at a rather early age, I was faced not only with the responsibility of loving and understanding my husband, my in-laws with whom I lived, and preparing for motherhood, but I was also faced with the responsibility of understanding, accepting, and loving new neighbors as well.

My new neighbors were of a different faith, from a different city with different interests, but still in spite of all our differences, we had to put up with each other, to maintain the friendship that is the expectation of our culture. I must admit this was quite a strain. It wasn't the cultural or religious difference that was difficult for me; it was that my new neighbors imposed on me and interfered in my life. They were loud and aggressive. I disliked so many things about them that made it difficult for me to have a loving attitude toward them. I looked into the depth of my being and I found only confusion. I really struggled with the commandment to love the neighbor and to live in the spirit of my faith. It was not easy. Even when I succeeded in caring about them, new questions came to mind. Didn't I and my family have a right to privacy? How could I guard my children from the values of these neighbors with whom I disagreed? Accepting and meeting the needs of these neighbors so often meant excluding other neighbors and their needs. Is this what God requires of me? Having next-door neighbors I did not like but was supposed to love was a challenge I have kept with me. It is probably a common challenge for us all.

Eventually these neighbors moved away and my husband and I moved with our family to live on the campus of the Friends School where we lived for eighteen years. There I had no next-door neighbors. Who, then, was my neighbor? The meaning of the circle of neighbors widened. My neighbor was any person who is in need and whom I might help. When Jesus taught of the importance of neighbors, it was and still is a radical teaching. If we are used to affirming the love of our family or perhaps the love of our clan or tribe or city, then we might spare a little love for neighbors.

However, the rich young lawyer who asked Jesus, "Who is my neighbor?" was bewildered to find that the real neighbor in the parable of the Good Samaritan was the stranger who had never seen the man in need before. The neighbor was a total stranger. Jesus showed him that a neighborhood is not just a location, it is the creation of a kind heart. A neighbor is one who discovers opportunities to do what God requires of the heart, no matter at what price or cost.

What a difficult lesson. If, as a Quaker, I try to see the light that is of God in each person, there are literally countless neighbors to tend to. There are near neighbors across the street and distant neighbors across the world. Without accepting limitations, it was inevitable that I felt frustrated and exhausted, sometimes even morally paralyzed. I decided some doors have to be closed, some roads not traveled, some needs not met, and some aspirations not achieved.

Love Your Enemies

The challenge of Jesus was not just loving one's neighbors. Add to that the challenge of loving one's enemies. G. K. Chesterton once said, "The Bible charges us to love our neighbors and our enemies probably because they are the same people." How true this is. Many of my neighbors who share the same land of Palestine—its wealth, history, and tradition, its sky, sun, fruits, and vegetables—are the national enemies of my people. My neighbors are Israelis, who occupy my homeland, who deny me freedom of self-determination, of expression, who deprive me and my children of our identity, and who beat up our students when they demonstrate against occupation. My neighbors are the same people who deported my brother-in-law and prevented my only brother from returning to his home.

My neighbors include the Israeli military governor of our area and his assistant. Years ago, they used to visit us in the school on many occasions, just to impress their presence upon us and our students. I tried to entertain them like friends in spite of their roles, but I felt the conflicting sense of responsibility—to maintain my sense of moral identity and integrity and at the same time to love my enemies, who happen to be my neighbors as well.

One day our students were on a strike. They were protesting against the ill treatment of other students in town and the mistreatment of Palestinian political prisoners. The military governor and his assistant came to our school to check on what was going on. Our oldest son was at home, as were also many of his classmates. The governor demanded to visit classrooms and check attendance. He then sent for five of our older students for interrogation and asked them to be at the military headquarters by four o' clock in the afternoon.

My husband and I were not happy about that, but still we had the responsibility and, I think, the opportunity to be neighbors to these visitors. I made tea, and my son, with some irony, said, "Mother, which tea cups would you like me to bring for the governor?" I said, "Our best golden brown cups that you gave me for Mother's Day. Come and fill also a plate with fresh homemade cookies and take them to your dad's office." My son was astonished. "Mother, how can I do this? I am on strike because I disapprove of all that the military governor does. Should I go and offer him tea and cookies?" "You don't have to," I said. "I will go. He is our guest, our neighbor, even if we dislike so many things about him." My son was convinced. He carried the tray up to the office and served them tea, but when he came back he was very depressed. He said, "Mother, who are our neighbors? The military authorities? Or all the other people around us who looked at me with distress in their eyes? Do you want all our people to lose their respect for us? How can Dad help them? Do you want our people to feel that we do not resist the evil that many of them have suffered? How can we assure our people that we love them?"

I was puzzled, confused, when the telephone bell rang. It was the voice of a mother full of fear and worry, the mother of one of our students who asked for my husband. "They have taken our sixteen-year-old son," she said. "They want his father to go and sign a statement that his son will never again share in any sit-in strikes or demonstrations." His father was too ill to go, and she even did not want him to know about her son's detention. She was anxious and frightened. "Maybe Mr. Zaru can do something. Please will you tell him?" I assured her I would.

With tears in my eyes I felt, then, that I had an answer for myself and for my son who wondered how we could serve tea to the military governor. The teachings are not simple rules as to what acts are required of us. To be a follower of Jesus is not to be relieved of the responsibility to think and act. What we know for sure is that in the complicated demands of any situation, we must respond to our neighbors, all of them, not in proportion to how we judge them to be worthy. They are our brothers, our sisters, and God's children, all of them—the military governor, the sixteen-year-old protester, and his terrified mother. We are asked by Christ to let the matter of cost be of least importance. My son and I finally agreed that in our situation no one can set rules for us to follow, but what we can do is to testify to the Spirit of God who leads us and gives us the needed guidance for every new situation.

On another occasion we had curfew for ten days. We were not allowed out at all. The janitor with his family, the gardener, and a teacher who was living in the school were close by. They used to sneak behind the bushes to visit with us and to share some of our food. I was faced again with the question of how to respond. Who is my neighbor when my food supply for my children is shrinking every day and I don't know how long the curfew will last? The gardener is single but he was more vocal and demanding than the janitor. My children loved and enjoyed the teacher's company more and they were begging him to stay for meals. Necessity is the mother of invention, so they say. I started cooking inventive meals for all of them with whatever I had of flour, rice, lentils, and other ingredients. This meant standing on my feet from dawn until sunset. My legs and back ached, I was exhausted, but I had a sense of joy and peace that I had succeeded in providing for my neighbors.

It would have been a perfect story, until I found out that one of these neighbors who enjoyed our ten days of hospitality did not really care about us. As soon as the curfew was lifted for a few hours, he disappeared to buy things for himself and did not even bother to ask if I needed anything that he might pick up for me, although he knew that at that point my husband was sick in bed. He felt God had entrusted him to us, but not us to him. He enjoyed having us as his neighbors but he did not bother to be a neighbor himself. Don't we often behave in the same way? Are we all not, at times, neighbors of convenience, able to forget our relatedness when times change?

Neighbors also appear in our lives and surprise us. Some years ago I had problems with my back and I had an operation in a hospital in Amman. I was away from home. I was helpless and the pain was more than I can describe. I had an aunt who lived in Amman. She is wealthy, chic, pretty, young, busy, and worldly. She would sometimes sacrifice her morning bridge game to visit me, to bring some food and to feed me, for I was unable to move. The nurses were few and I did not feel I could ring the bell to ask for help. A friend of my husband who went through the same operation asked the cleaning woman at his school if she could help me when she finished her duty. She was willing and came to my bedside. This woman was not related to me in any way. I had never seen her before. As a Muslim, she was from a different background and faith. Yet when she entered my room and I was alone in great pain she stood by, held my hand, and said, "Don't cry, your brother is the brother of all of us, so you are the sister of all." Then we heard the call for prayer, and she being a Muslim started praying in her own way saying, "God, look after your daughter." In the days that followed, I started addressing her as "auntie" in Arabic, which meant a real closeness. The nurses were confused. They could not figure out who was my real aunt. Clearly these two women could not be sisters. But the unrelated auntie stepped into my life as a neighbor and brought me closer to God and to herself.

Neighbors of All Faiths

As our shrinking world now makes us all near neighbors, I am increasingly aware of two facts about our new global village. One is that we are different from one another in race, culture, belief, and lifestyles. The other is that we are exceedingly alike. There is a wide range of common needs and desires, fears and hopes that bind us together in our humanness. The well-being of each one is intricately interrelated to the well-being of each other. Mutuality and interdependence are the necessities of our future.

As I have become more appreciative of the many friends and neighbors I have from different faiths, nationalities, and cultures, the law of neighborhood I grew up with has kept on expanding. Despite the walls and barriers of our lives as Palestinians, this wider sense of neighborhood has no walls or barriers around it. I have wonderful neighbors in many parts of the world, as well as in Ramallah. I have learned so much more about myself through these neighbors, for my attitude toward them has been a sign of the degree of my own self-knowledge. I started seeing in others that which my own spiritual experience has shown me about myself.

One thing I have learned from neighbors of other faiths is that "religion" is often a problem for all of us. Religion is *the* problem where its structures of dominance have oppressed us as Palestinians, as women, or as any other people who have been on the downside of religious chauvinism. Religion is also a solution where its vision of liberation or equality has generated powerful social and political movements for change.

The same religious traditions are often both a problem and a solution. Many people I meet across religious traditions have the same view: that "religion" can be dangerously institutional and can wield destructive power. Many of us have started to speak of what is "spiritual," to undermine the institutional resonance of "religion" with the breath of fresh air that comes with the "spirit." But remember, in the English language the meaning for religion is to bind, to tie, and to fasten. So religion can be the bond of kinship that binds us together and binds us to God. Religion includes those deeply held traditions and values that shape our ways of thinking and our hopes for change. Religion should also be spiritual in order to breathe life into a world weary of conflict.

I have also learned from my life of dialogue with others that religious truth is not the exclusive possession of anyone—not of any tradition, community, or person. Therefore, the diversity of communities, understandings, practices, and visions of God should not be obstacles for us to overcome, but opportunities for our engagement and dialogue with one another. For me, dialogue with Muslims, Jews, or others does not at all mean giving up my commitments as a Christian and a Quaker, but rather it means opening up those commitments to the give and take of real-time and real-world struggles.

Interdependence is the watchword of our era. Problems cannot be isolated from one another. World systems are interconnected, including the structures of globalization, such as banking, commerce, communications, and armaments. In the area of consciousness, world events have pressed upon us a sense of our global connections, whether in the development of a consumer mentality with its expectations and desires or the awareness of the ecological damage of careless industrialization.

More than ever, we human beings *really do* depend upon one another. My well-being and yours, my security and yours, my freedom and yours, my rights and yours are inseparable. Hearing one another in the mutuality of dialogue gives us the knowledge and wisdom to discern our close connections, to see the real implications of our situation, and to join together in positive and creative ways. As a Palestinian, I know full well that the people of Israel are not freer than we are. Both Israelis and Palestinians live in fear. Neither Israelis nor Palestinians have peace. Both Israelis and Palestinians yearn for security. Others cannot give us freedom, peace, and security. No government, no army, no wall no matter how long or high will provide for us what can only be supplied by the cultivation of mutuality and trust.

What will bring us peace is inward transformation that will lead to outward action. Our miseries are not going to stop by condemnation or disapproval, and certainly not by barbed wire, rockets, and bombs. If we see the urgency for real transformation, only then will we transform ourselves. Peace will come when we have made the costly decision to be at peace with our neighbors. We cannot live a day without saying yes or no for death or for life, for war or for peace, injustice or justice. The choice is ours. To postpone or evade the decision is to decide.

In the Christian tradition, we use the image of the human body to describe our relationship with one another—not only to our friends and relatives, but to all our neighbors. We are all members of the one body, as Paul tells us in 1 Corinthians. We are not alike, just as the parts of the body are not alike, but we belong together. If one is hurt, all suffer, just as my whole body seems to suffer from the pain, in my back. We live in a world in which more than half the population is hurt by hunger, poverty, ignorance, oppression, pollution, or war. Is this not our pain too? We are all involved in humankind because we all *are* humankind.

I speak of family and friends gathered in the sunlight in my Ramallah living room in their symbolic ways as bearers of the light of God, a light that is within each person. It is the light I have tried to protect and nurture within myself. The more I can see it within myself, the more clearly I can recognize that light in others. People in other traditions speak of human worth and Divine Presence in different ways—as spirit, or soul, or conscience. To be human is to recognize the precious value of every human being. How we speak of this recognition, this consciousness is not so important. But living in this consciousness will enable us to discover what it is to be real neighbors in a world of real differences.

NOTES

Editor's Introduction

1. David Shulman, *Dark Hope: Working for Peace in Israel-Palestine* (Chicago: University of Chicago Press, 2007), 66.

1. What Life Do I Lead?

1. Jay Murphy, "Peace When?" *In These Times*, May 13, 1996, in a review of Edward W. Said's *Peace and Its Discontents*.

2. Edward W. Said, "Winners and Losers—July 1994," in *Peace and Its Discontents: Gaza-Jericho 1993–1995* (London: Vintage, 1995), 73–83.

2. *Al Nakba,* the Catastrophe

1. On this occasion, I had also been invited by the Church of Sweden to speak in the Cathedral of Lund and the Cathedral of Stockholm.

2. I. F. Stone, *Underground to Palestine and Reflections Thirty Years Later* (London: Hutchinson and Co., 1979), 235–60.

3. Human Rights

1. World Bank, *Twenty-Seven Months—Intifada, Closures, and Palestinian Economic Crisis: An Assessment* (Washington, D.C.: World Bank, May 2003), xiv.

2. Abbas Shiblak, "Residency Status and Civil Rights of Palestinian Refugees in Arab Countries," *Journal of Palestine Studies* 25, no. 3 (Spring 1996): 36–45.

3. United Nations Development Programme, *Arab Human Development Report 2004: Towards Freedom in the Arab World* (New York: UNDP/RBAS, 2005), 30.

4. United Nations Office for Coordination of Humanitarian Affairs (OCHA), U.N. Relief and Works Agency for Palestine Refugees (UNRWA), *The Humanitarian Impact of the West Bank Barrier on Palestinian Communities*, 31 March 2005, 6.

5. United Nations Office for Coordination of Humanitarian Affairs (OCHA), PowerPoint Presentation, August 2007.

6. United Nations Office for Coordination of Humanitarian Affairs (OCHA), "The Humanitarian Impact on Palestinians of Israeli Settlements and other Infrastructure in the West Bank," July 2007.

4. Jerusalem: *Al-Quds,* the Holy

1. Amos Gvirtz, "Don't say we didn't know," Number 92, Israeli Committee Against House Demolitions, December 2007.

2. Jane Lampman, "New Constraints Squeeze Churches in Holy Land," *Christian Science Monitor*, 4 May 2004, 96 (111): 1.

7. War, Peace, and Justice

1. *News from Within*, October 1999, from The Alternative Information Center http://www.alternativenews.org/aic-publications/news-from-within, accessed March 31, 2008.

2. Edward W. Said, "How do you spell apartheid? O-S-L-O," *Ha'aretz,* October 11, 1998.

3. Maher Bitar, "Water and the Palestinian-Israeli Conflict: Competition or Cooperation?" Foundation for Middle East Peace, December 22, 2005.

8. What I Owe My Muslim Neighbor

1. *The Koran*, translated from the Arabic by J. M. Rodwell, M.A., 1861 (Dutton, N.Y.: Everyman's Library, 1971).

9. Solidarity with Women

1. It is true that in the passage in Colossians, which has somewhat similar material, the injunction "to be subordinate" is used of wives to husbands. In

that place the sentence reads "Wives, be subordinate to your husbands as is fitting in the Lord" (Col. 3.18). But here we are dealing with a different text, and a different mode of expression.

10. Neighbors

1. Nayler is quoted in the 1963 Swarthmore Lecture by L. Hugh Doncaster, *God in Everyman* (Kent, England: Headley Brothers Ltd., 1963), 3–4.

REFERENCES AND SOURCES

I N A DYNAMIC SITUATION, many of the citations and statistics over
the years of these essays have understandably changed. The following
resources provide information on many of the topics treated in these
essays. All Web sites have been accessed and are active as of April 10,
2008, unless otherwise noted.

General Sources

- B'Tselem, The Israeli Information Center for Human Rights
  in the Occupied Territories, has up-to-date information about
  most of the topics addressed here. http://www.btselem.org/
  english/About_BTselem/Index.asp
- United Nations, Office of the High Commissioner for Human
  Rights.
- http://www.ohchr.org/EN/Pages/WelcomePage.aspx
- United Nations Development Programme, *Arab Human Development Report.* http://www.undp.org/arabstates/ahdr2005.shtml
- The Palestinian Diaspora and Refugee Center. http://www.shaml.
  org (as of April 10, 2008, this Web site is under reconstruction)
- The United Nations Relief and Works Agency for Palestinian
  Refugees in the Near East. http://www.un.org/unrwa/

- The United Nations Information System on the Question of Palestine. http://domino.un.org/unispal.nsf/frontpage5!OpenPage
- The World Council of Churches. http://www.oikoumene.org/

Demographics

The Number of Palestinians Worldwide, in the West Bank and Gaza, and in Israel

- The Jewish Virtual Library claims that population of Palestinians worldwide numbered over 8.8 million as of mid-2001. http://jewishvirtuallibrary.org/jsource/arabs/palpoptotal.html
- The Web site All About Palestine claims the population of Palestinians worldwide numbered 9.3 million as of January 2003, citing the Palestine Central Bureau of Statistics as its source. http://www.allaboutpalestine.com/index.shtml
- Table 2.1 of the "Statistical Abstract of Israel 2006" claims the population of Israel as of 2005 is 6,990,700 people. It also claims there are 1,377,100 Arab Israeli citizens as of 2005. This is about 20 percent of Israel's population. The abstract is a product of Israel's Central Bureau of Statistics. http://www1.cbs.gov.il/reader/
- The Israel Ministry of Foreign Affairs Web site claims there are over 5 million Jewish Israeli citizens. The non-Jewish population, which is primarily Arab, is 23 percent of Israel's population and numbers 1.5 million people. The total population of Israel, then, is 6.5 million people. http://www.mfa.gov.il/MFA
- Mark Tessler, *A History of the Israeli-Palestinian Conflict* (Bloomington: Indiana University Press, 1994) claims that the population of West Bank and Gaza in 1967 was approximately 1,260,000 people.
- The United Nations Population Fund website claims that as of 2005, there are 3.5 million people living in the occupied

Palestinian territories (OPT). http://www.unfpa.org/profile/palestinianterritory.cfm

- The Population Reference Bureau numbers the population of OPT at 3.9 million as of mid-2006. http://www.prb.org/Countries/PalestinianTerritory.aspx

Palestinian Christians: Their Diminishing Numbers in Palestine and Jerusalem

- Hilal Khashan, "Arab Christians as Symbol," *The Middle East Quarterly* 8, no. 1 (Winter 2001), says there are fewer than 12 million Christians in the Arab-speaking world. http://www.meforum.org/article/4

- Wikipedia's article "Arab Christians" estimates 17.5 million Arab Christians in the Middle East. http://en.wikipedia.org/wiki/Arab_Christians

- "Palestinian Christian leader calls for comprehensive peace settlement," *Ekklesia* (February 4, 2007), notes that there are 42,000 Palestinian Christians living in the OPT occupied Palestinian territories, making up less than 2 percent of the overall OPT population. http://www.ekklesia.co.uk/content/news_syndication/article_07024younan.shtml

- Megan Goldin, "Holy Land's Christians caught in the midst of conflict," *Relief Web* (Reuters) (April 12 2006) notes that there are about 50,000 Christians in OPT, which is about 1.5 percent of the population. http://www.reliefweb.int/rw/RWB.NSF/db900SID/SODA-6NS3Q9?OpenDocument&rc=3&emid=ACOS-635PFR

- Corrine Whitlatch, "Palestinian Christians Receive Attention and Reveal Vulterability," *Quartery Policy Analysis Newsletter* (Summer 2006), states that as of January 2005 there were 8,000 indigenous Christians living in Jerusalem. http://www.cmep.org/newsletter/2006June.htm

- Jane Lampman, "New Constraints Squeeze Churches in Holy Land," *Christian Science Monitor* 96, no. 111 (May 4, 2004): 1. http://www.csmonitor.com/2004/0504/p01s04-wome.html

Residency Rights

- Abbas Shiblak, "Residency Status and Civil Rights of Palestinian Refugees in Arab Countries," *Palestinian Diaspora and Refugee Centre*, claims that since 1967, approximately 150,000 people have lost residency rights. http://www.shaml.org/publications/monos/mono1.htm#Residency%20Status:%20A%20Case%20of%20Uncertainty (as of April 10, 2008, this Web site is under reconstruction)

- "East Jerusalem: Legal Status of East Jerusalem and its Residents," *B'Tselem.* http://www.btselem.org/english/Jerusalem/Legal_Status.asp

The Settlements

Numbers and Impact

- B'Tselem claims that as of December 31, 2004, there were 418,305 settlers in the West Bank, including East Jerusalem. It also says that Israel's Interior Ministry recognizes 152 settlements in the West Bank and the Gaza Strip. The site does note, though, that there are many outposts that, although the Interior Ministry does not recognize them as such, are settlements. http://www.btselem.org/English/Settlements/Index.asp (click on "Settlement population, XLS" for population statistics)

The Wall and Its Impact

- U.N. Office for Coordination of Humanitarian Affairs (OCHA), U.N. Relief and Works Agency for Palestine Refugees (UNRWA),

The Humanitarian Impact of the West Bank Barrier on Palestinian Communities (March 31, 2005), 6.

* "Legal Consequences of the Construction of a Wall in the Occupied Palestinian Territory," *Organization of the Islamic Conference*, January 2004. http://domino.un.org/unispal.nsf/3576688 78a81e92785256df9005c23c2/2db345faba654d4585256eb6006 6c514!OpenDocument

Punitive House Demolitions
* Ronen Shnayderman, "Through No Fault of Their Own: Punitive House Demolitions during the al-Aqsa Intifada," ed. Yehezkel Lein, *B'Tselem* (November 2004). http://209.85.165.104/ search?q=cache:q88b2wc0gtAJ:www.btselem.org/ Download/200411_Punitive_House_Demolitions_Eng.doc+ houses+damaged+and+demolished+since+2000&hl=en&ct=cl nk&cd=1&gl=us&lr=lang_en&inlang=en
* U.N. Relief and Works Agency for Palestine Refugees (UNRWA), *Supplementary Appeal for Rafah* (June 30, 2004), 4.

Water Issues
* "The Water Crisis: Gap in Water Consumption," *B'Tselem*. The organization claims that per capita water consumption in the West Bank is approximately 60 liters per person per day, whereas in Israeli a person consumes approximately 280 liters each day. http://www.btselem.org/english/Water/Consumption_Gap.asp
* Kathy Kamphoefner, "Water Inequalities," *Peace Work Magazine* (November 15, 2002). Kamphoefner cites an article found in *Ha'aretz* that stated that 80 percent of water from the West Bank and Gaza goes to Israelis with the remaining 20 percent left for Palestinians. http://www.peaceworkmagazine.org/ pwork/0211/021115.htm

Prisoners

- B'Tselem claims that 9,103 Palestinians are in Israeli detention. It does not say what the reason is for holding these prisoners. http://www.btselem.org/english/statistics/Detainees_and_ Prisoners.asp

- B'Tselem's Web site says that as of January 2007 there are 800 people in administrative detention. http://www.btselem.org/ english/Administrative_Detention/Statistics.asp

- The Mandela Institute for Human Rights-Palestine claims 10,580 Palestinians are in Israeli prisons (as of 2006), and that 383 of these prisoners are minors. http://mandela-palestine.org

ABOUT THE AUTHOR

J EAN ZARU was born in Ramallah, Palestine, in 1940, eight years before the Palestinian diaspora. Her life has been devoted to dialogue and nonviolent social change.

As a Palestinian woman living under military occupation and at the same time finding herself in a traditional culture, her life has been nothing less than an active engagement in the struggle for liberation— liberation for Palestinians, for women, and for all peoples. She has done this through work in her own community, as well as regionally and internationally.

Jean is the presiding clerk of the Ramallah Friends Meeting in Palestine and has served in that capacity for over nineteen years. Currently, Jean is spearheading an effort with an international steering committee to restore the historic meetinghouse and establish an International Friends Center with the aim of contributing to the building of a culture of peace and nonviolence in Palestine.

For thirteen years, Jean was a teacher of religion and ethics at the Ramallah Friends School, where her husband, Fuad, served as principal. In addition, Jean serves as a volunteer consultant and resource person for many faith-based organizations, including church-related development agencies. She served as a member of the Central Committee of the World Council of Churches, as well as on their Working Group for Interfaith Dialogue. She has been president of the YWCA Jerusalem and vice-president of the World YWCA.

In 1992, Jean was a visiting scholar at Hartford Seminary in Connecticut, and the next year was Dorothy Cadbury Fellow at Selly Oaks

College, United Kingdom. Among her numerous awards and recognitions are the Swedish Fellowship of Reconciliation Peace Award in 2004 and that organization's Non-Violence Award in 2005. She has been the keynote speaker at numerous conferences around the world and her papers have been published in many books and journals. She continues to struggle for human rights and women's rights and continues her work in interfaith dialogue with other persons of faith.

Lightning Source UK Ltd.
Milton Keynes UK
21 May 2010
154428UK00001B/64/P